This Work Is Dedicated To
My *Best Friend* Lois
My Wife

Contents

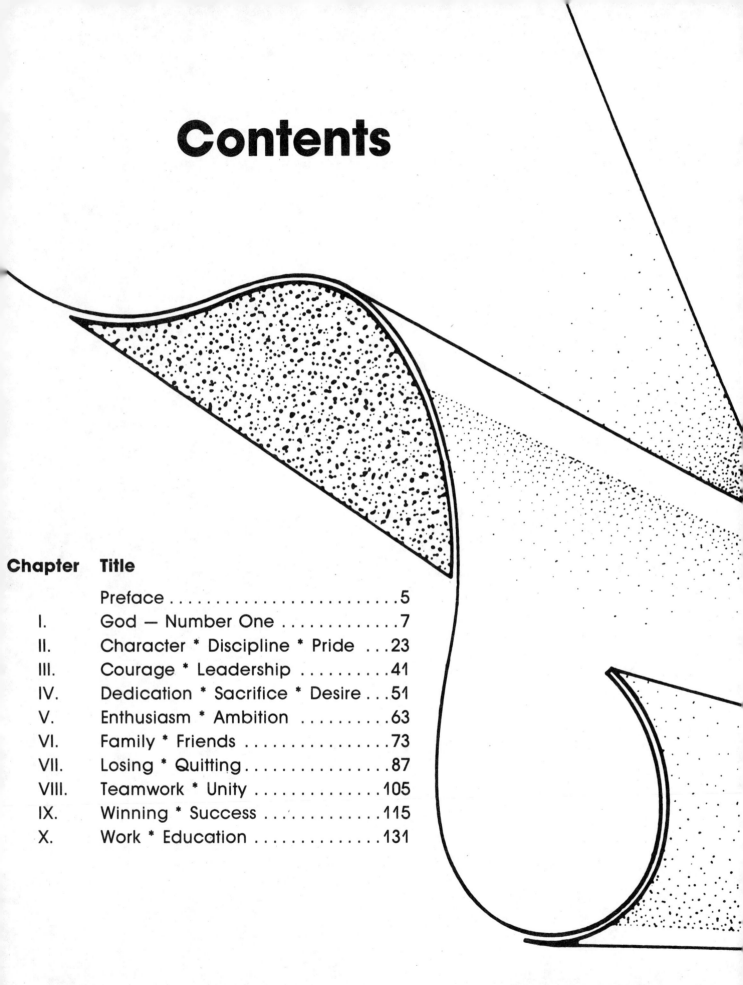

Chapter	Title	
	Preface	5
I.	God — Number One	7
II.	Character * Discipline * Pride	23
III.	Courage * Leadership	41
IV.	Dedication * Sacrifice * Desire	51
V.	Enthusiasm * Ambition	63
VI.	Family * Friends	73
VII.	Losing * Quitting	87
VIII.	Teamwork * Unity	105
IX.	Winning * Success	115
X.	Work * Education	131

Preface

Words both written and spoken, have played an enormous role in the history of man. Some people have been gifted with the ability to put words into use that move others to great accomplishments.

Generals, presidents, teachers, philosophers and coaches have had to call on words to inspire their charges. In this book I have tried to organize, by subject, some of the quotes, poems and one liners that I have collected and found useful over the past 20 years as a coach and teacher.

We frequently forget the power of words and use them to hurt rather than help. I hope my collection will be of some aid in the latter.

I would like to apologize to any originator to whom I have failed to give credit and to anyone who I gave credit not deserved.

Tiger Ellison delivered a speech to the National Football Coaches Association, concerning "Why Coach?" He closed his talk with this poem which sums up my feelings about this book:

An old man going a lone highway
Came at the evening cold and gray
To a chasm vast and deep and wide,
Through which was flowing a swollen tide.
The old man crossed in the twilight dim
That swollen stream held no fears for him
But he paused when safe on the other side
And built a bridge to span the tide.
"Old man," saaid a fellow pilgrim near,
"You are wasting strength with building here.
Your journey will end with the ending day;
You never again must pass this way.
You have crossed the chasm deep and wide;
Why build you the bridge at the eventide?
The builder lifted his old gray head,
"Good friend, in the path I have come," he said,
"There followeth after me today
A youth whose feet must pass this way.
This swollen stream which was naught to me
To that fair haired youth may a pitfall be.
He, too, must cross in the twilight dim.
Good friend, I am building the bridge for him."

Winning Words

Chapter I

God

I. GOD

God Chooses Ordinary Men For Extraordinary Work

* * *

God's Hall of Fame

Your name may not appear down here
  In this world's hall of fame.
In fact you may be so unknown
  That no one knows your name

The All Stars here may pass you by
  On neon lights of blue,
But if you love and serve the Lord,
  Then I have good news for you.

This hall of fame is only good
  As long as time shall be,
But keep in mind God's hall of fame
  Is for eternity.

To have your name inscribed up there
  Is greater yet by far
Than all the halls of fame down here
  And every man-made star.

This crowd on earth may soon forget
  The heroes of the past.
They cheer like mad until you fall
  And that's how long you last.

But God, He never does forget
  And in His hall of fame,
By just believing in His Son
  Inscribed you'll find your name.

I tell you, friend, I wouldn't trade
  My name however small,
That written there beyond the stars
  In that celestial hall.

For any famous name on earth
  Or glory that they share
I'd rather be an unknown here
  And have my name up there.

* * *

Lord, help me to remember that nothing is going to happen to me today
that You and I can't handle.

* * *

"*BELIEF* IS THE THERMOSTAT WHICH REGULATES *SUCCESS*"

I. GOD

DO YOU NOT KNOW THAT YOU ARE GOD'S TEMPLE
AND THAT GOD'S SPIRIT DWELLS IN YOU?

1 Cor. 3:16

* * *

An athlete is not crowned unless he competes according to the rules.

2 Timothy 2:5

* * *

I CAN OF MINE OWNSELF DO NOTHING.

John 5:30

* * *

You cannot love **God** without loving every fellow creature He made. An act of contempt or rejection or injustice or neglect toward the least, the lowest, the dumbest, the poorest - is an act against Him.

If Christianity does not mean this, it means nothing.

* * *

WHEN YOU'RE READY TO QUIT AND TO GIVE UP THE FIGHT,
AND THE SKIES ALL ABOVE YOU ARE BLACK AS THE NIGHT,
THEN LIFT UP YOUR HAND AND THROUGH THE OWLY NIGHT AIR,
THERE IS POWER AND TRIUMPH IN CONFIDENT PRAYER.

* * *,

Do not pray for an easy life. Pray to be a **strong person.**

* * *

IN A RACE, EVERYONE RUNS BUT ONLY ONE PERSON GETS THE PRIZE.
SO, RUN YOUR RACE TO WIN.

1 Cor. 9:24

* * *

When a man has a great deal given to him,
a great deal will be demanded of him.

Luke 12:48

* * *

"WHEN THE ONE GREAT SCORER COMES TO MARK AGAINST YOUR
NAME HE WRITES — NOT THAT YOU WON OR LOST — BUT
HOW YOU PLAYED THE GAME."

I. GOD

Dear Lord,

In this battle that goes on through life, I ask but a field that is fair. A chance to compete with all in the strife. And courage to strive and dare.

And if I should win, let it be by this code. With my faith and my honor held high. And if I should lose, let me stand by the road. And cheer as the winner goes by.

* * *

GOD, GRANT THAT I MAY LIVE TO FISH UNTIL MY DYING DAY — AND WHEN IT COMES TO MY LAST CAST, I THEN MOST HUMBLY PRAY — WHEN IN THE LORD'S SAFE NET I'M PEACEFULLY ASLEEP, THAT IN HIS MERCY I BE JUDGED BIG ENOUGH TO KEEP.

A. BURHAM

* * *

He who spends some time on his knees
has no trouble standing on his feet.

* * *

Let us not pray to be sheltered from dangers but to be
fearless when facing them.

* * *

ABRAHAM LINCOLN DURING THE DARKEST HOURS OF THE CIVIL WAR, IN RESPONSE TO THE QUESTION WHETHER HE WAS SURE GOD WAS "ON OUR SIDE"
"I do not know: I have not thought about that. But I am very anxious to know whether we are on *God's Side.*"

* * *

The *Lord* sometimes takes us into troubled waters
not to drown but to cleanse us. . .

* * *

Dear Lord As We Huddle Here
Help Us To See It Clear,
That Playing Hard And Playing Fair,
Is What We Are Asking Everywhere.

* * *

Dear Father,

Our one great coach, help us to play this game with dedicated spirit and willing body. With open and eager mind. So the lessons learned as we compete today may better prepare us for life's long way.

I. GOD

GOD'S HELP IS JUST A PRAYER AWAY

* * *

Footprints

One night a man had a dream, he dreamed he was walking along the beach with the Lord. Across the sky flashed scenes from his life. For each scene he noticed two sets of footprints in the sand — one belonging to him — the other belonging to the Lord.

When the last scene of his life flashed before him, he looked back at the footprints in the sand. He noticed that many times along the path of life there was only one set of footprints. He also noticed that it happened at the very lowest and saddest time in his life. This really bothered him and he questioned the Lord about it. "Lord, you said that once I decided to follow you, you would walk with me all the way. But, I have noticed that during the most troublesome times in my life there is only one set of footprints. I don't understand why in times when I needed you most, you would leave me." The Lord replied, "my precious, precious child, I love you and I would never, never leave you during your times of trial and suffering, when you see only one set of footprints, it was then that I carried you."

* * *

My *God* is first, my *Team* is second, and *I* am third.

* * *

Lord, when we are wrong, make us willing to change. And when we are right, make us easy to live with.

* * *

—Take Time—

Take Time to think -
it is the source of power.

Take Time to play -
it is the secret of youth.

Take Time to read -
it is the foundation of wisdom.

Take Time to pray -
it is the greatest power on earth.

Take Time to love and be loved -
it is a God given privilege.

Take Time to be friendly -
it is the road to happiness.

Take Time to laugh -
it is the music of the soul.

I. GOD

A MAN'S PRAYER — Grantland Rice

Let me live, oh Mighty Master, such a life as men shall know.
Tasting triumph and disaster, joy and not too much woe;

Let me run the gamut over, let me fight and love and laugh, and when I'm
beneath the clover let this be my epitaph:

Here lies one who took his chances in the busy world of men; battled luck
and circumstances fought and fell and fought again;

Won sometimes, but did no crowing, lost sometimes, but did not wail, took
his beating, but kept going, never let his courage fail.

He was fallible and human, therefore loved and understood both his fellow
man and woman, whether good or not so good;

Kept his spirit undiminished, never lay down on a friend, played the game
until it was finished, lived a sportsman to the end. . .

* * *

TALENT IS GOD GIVEN — *BE THANKFUL*
FAME IS MAN GIVEN — *BE HUMBLE*
CONCEIT IS SELF GIVEN — *BE CAREFUL*

* * *

THE COMMITTED MAN — By Vince Lombardi

"We know how rough the road will be, how heavy here the load will be,
we know about the barricades that wait along the track
but we have set our soul ahead upon a certain goal ahead
and nothing left from hell to sky shall ever turn us back."

* * *

Do the very best you can, and leave the outcome to God.

* * *

I shall pass through this world but once. Any good that I can do, or any kindness that I can show any human being, let me do it now and not defer it, for
I shall not pass this way again.

* * *

WE WERE NOT PUT ON THIS EARTH BY GOD TO MAKE A *LIVING*
BUT TO MAKE A *LIFE.*

I. GOD

"God will look us over not for medals, or diplomas, or degrees: BUT FOR SCARS."
Edward Sheldon

* * *

"CLIMB 'TIL YOUR DREAM COMES TRUE"

Often your tasks will be many, and more than you think you can do—
Often the road will be rugged and the hills insurmountable, too—
But always remember, the hills ahead are never as steep as they seem,
And with faith in your heart start upward and climb 'til you reach your dream,
For nothing in life that is worthy is ever too hard to achieve,
If you have the courage to try it and you have the faith to believe-
For faith is a force that is greater than knowledge or power or skill,
And many defeats turn to triumph if you trust in God's wisdom and will-
For faith is a mover of mountains, there's nothing that God cannot do-
So start out today with faith in your heart and "CLIMB 'TIL YOUR DREAMS COME TRUE!

Helen Steiner Rice

* * *

What you are is God's gift to you —
what you make of yourself is your gift to God.

* * *

SLOW ME DOWN LORD

Slow me down Lord, ease the pounding of my heart by the quieting of my mind. Steady my hurried pace with a vision of the eternal reach of time.

Give me amid the confusion of the day, the calmness of the everlasting hills.
Break the tensions of my nerves and muscles with the soothing music of the singing streams that live in my memory, help me to know the magical, restoring power of sleep.

Teach me the art of taking minute vacations, of slowing down to look at a flower, to chat with a friend, to pat a dog, to read a few lines from a good book.

Slow me down Lord, and inspire me to send my roots deep into the soil of life's enduring values that I may grow toward the stars to my greater destiny.

I. GOD

The Station

Tucked away in our subconscious is an idyllic vision. We see ourselves on a long trip that spans the continent. We are traveling by train. Out the windows, we drink in the passing scene of cars on nearby highways, of children waving at a crossing, of cattle grazing on a distant hillside, of smoke pouring from a power plant, of row upon row of corn and wheat, of flat lands and valleys, of mountains and rolling hillsides, of city skylines and village hills.

But uppermost in our minds is the final destination. On a certain day at a certain hour we will pull into the station. Bands will be playing and flags will be waving. Once we get there so many wonderful dreams will come true, and pieces of our lives will fit together like a completed jigsaw puzzle. How restlessly we paced the aisles, damning the minutes for loitering - waiting, waiting, waiting for the station.

"When we reach the station, that will be it." we cry. "When I'm 18, "When I buy a new 450SL Mercedes Benz!" "When I put the last kid through college" "When I reach the age of retirement, I shall live happily ever after!"

Sooner or later we must realize there is no station, no one place to arrive at once and for all. The true joy of life is the trip. The station is only dream. It constantly outdistances us.

"Relish the moment" is a good motto, especially when coupled with Psalm 118:24: "This is the day which the Lord hath made; we will rejoice and be glad in it." It isn't the burdens of today that drive men mad. It's the regrets over yesterday and the fear of tomorrow. Regret and fear are twin thieves that rob us of today.

So, stop pacing the aisles and counting the miles. Instead, climb more mountains, eat more ice cream, go barefoot more often, swim more rivers, watch more sunsets, laugh more, cry less. Life must be lived as we go along. The station will come soon enough.

* * *

God gave us two ends to use:
one to think with -
the other to sit with -
Success depends on which one you choose:
heads you'll win
tails you'll lose.

* * *

ANGER IS OFTEN MORE HARMFUL THAN THE INJURY THAT CAUSED IT.

I. GOD

Dear Lord,

We pray for strength both on and off the field, and when we are faced with problems, to evil never yield, but keep our goal in sight and play with all our might. . .

* * *

"Dear God: Help me to be a sport in this little game of life. I don't ask for any place in the line-up; play me where you need me. I only ask for the stuff to give you a hundred percent of what I've got. If all the hard drives come my way, I thank you for the compliment. Help me to remember that you won't let anything come that you and I can't handle. And help me to take the bad breaks as part of the game. Help me to be thankful for them.

And **God,** help me always to play on the square, no matter what the other players do. Help me to see that often the best part of the game is helping others. Help me to be a "regular friend" with the other players.

Finally, **God**, if fate seems to uppercut me with both hands and I'm laid up on the shelves in sickness or old age, help me to take that as part of the game also. Help me not to wimper or squeal that the game was unfair or that I had a raw deal. When in the dusk I get the final whistle, I ask for no lying, complimentary stones. I'd only like to know that you feel I did my best."

Chaplain's Digest

* * *

A Football Coach's Prayer

I suppose I should ask for flashy backs whose hips are in constant swivel and whose speed and dash make people say "Boy, they run to beat the Devil."

I ought to include a massive line with chassis like big Mack trucks, whose brute strength scares all opponents and drops them like sitting ducks.

I could ask for a team with precision, whose efforts would all honors take and also plead for a squad with brains who would never make a mistake.

But Lord, I am an understandable coach - the talent cannot be all mine - so if you give me the things I ask for, I'll never complain or whine.

Just give me a bunch of eager boys with the spirit to fight and win, who will battle as soon as they take the field and most of all will never give in!

* * *

I. GOD

THE BIGGEST GAME OF ALL

Life is a game of football,
And you play it every day.
It isn't just the breaks you get.
But how well you play.
Stop and look the whole team over,
You've some pretty rugged men
If you work them all together,
There's no goal you can't defend.
Your fullback's name is **Courage**
You need him in this game.
For **Truth** and **Faith**, your halfbacks,
There'll be many yards to gain.
Your quarterback is very fast,
Though small and hard to see.
So watch Son, when he gets the ball,
He's **Opportunity.**
At right end there's Religion
He's stood the test of time.
At left end there is **Brotherhood.**
He's the bulwark of the line.
Your right tackle is **Ambition.**
Don't ever let him shirk.
Left tackle is a husky man,
You'll find his name is **Work.**
Your left guard's name is **Humor**
He's important to the team.
While **Honor's** playing right guard
Your game is alway clean.
If **Love** plays at the center spot
and does his very best
Then you shall have a winning team,
And really know success.

The other team is strong, Son.
Greed, Envy, Hatred, and **Deceit**
Are four strong backs you'll have to buck
To ward off sure defeat.
Discouragement and **Falsehood**
Are the big boys on the end.
You'll have to tackle hard my boy,
When you meet up with these men.
Selfishness and **Jealousy,**
You'll find them playing guard.
While **Carelessness** and a man called **Waste**
Are tackles you can't disregard.
There's one more man you'll have to watch
All through the game, my dear,
He's playing center for the team,
I'm told his name is **Fear.**
This game will not be easy;
There'll be struggle, there'll be strife
As you work for victory glorious
In this real tough game of life.
So stand behind your team, Son.
There'll be many who'll applaud.
Just remember you're the Captain;
And the Referee is God.

I. GOD

Found on the Body of a Confederate Soldier

"I asked for **strength** — that I might achieve.
 He made me weak — that I might obey.
I asked for **health** — that I might do greater things.
 I was given grace — that I might do better things.
I asked for **riches** — that I might be happy.
 I was given poverty — that I might be wise.
I asked for **power** — that I might have the praise of men.
 I was given weakness — that I might feel the need of God.
I asked for **all things** that I might enjoy life.
 I was given life — that I might enjoy all things.
I received nothing that I asked for — and all that I hoped for.
 My prayer was answered."

* * *

God's Minute

I have only just a minute,
 only sixty seconds in it,
forced upon me, can't refuse it,
didn't seek it, didn't choose it,
 but it's up to me to use it.

It may suffer if I lose it,
 give account if I abuse it,
Just a tiny little minute,
 but eternity is in it.

* * *

"Thank God every morning when you get up that you have something to do which must be done, whether you like it or not. Being forced to do your best will breed in you temperance, self-control, diligence, strength of will, content, and a hundred other virtues which the idle never know."

* * *

*The most valuable gift you can give another
is a good example.*

* * *

WOMAN. . . Was made from the rib of man. She was not created from his head to top him, nor his feet to be stepped upon.
She was made from his side — to be equal to him, from beneath his arm — to be protected by him, near his heart — to be loved by him.

I. GOD

A COACH'S PRAYER

Build me an athlete, O Lord, who will be strong enough to know when he is weak and brave enough to face himself when he is afraid, one who will be proud and unbending in honest defeat and humble and gentle in victory.

Build me an athlete whose wishbone will not be where his backbone should be, an athlete who will know Thee and that to know himself is the foundation stone of knowledge. Lead him, I pray, not in the path of ease and comfort, but under the stress and spur of difficulties and challenge. Here let him learn to stand up in the storm; here let him learn compassion for those who fall.

Build me an athlete whose heart will be clear, whose goal will be high; an athlete who will master himself before he seeks to master other men; one who will learn to laugh, yet never forget how to weep; one who will reach into the future yet never forget the past. And after all these things are his, add, I pray, enough of a sense of humor, never to take himself too seriously. Give him humility, so that he may always remember the simplicity of true greatness, the open mind of true wisdom, the meekness of true strength. Then, I, his coach, will dare to whisper, "I have not lived in vain."

* * *

Lord, make me an instrument of your peace,
    where there is hatred. . .let me sow love;
    where there is injury. . .pardon;
    where there is doubt. . .faith;
    where there is despair. . .hope;
    where there is darkness. . .light;
    where there is sadness. . .joy;
O Divine Master, grant that I may not so much seek
    to be consoled. . .as to console;
    to be understood. . .as to understand;
    to be loved. . .as to love;
For it is in the giving. . .that we receive;
It is in the pardoning. . .that we are pardoned;
It is in the dying. . .that we are born to eternal life.

        Saint Francis

* * *

The coach knocked on the pearly gates
His face grim and old
He stood before the Man of fate
For admission to the fold
What have you done
St. Peter said to gain admission here
I've been a football coach he said
For many and many a year
The pearly gates swung open wide
St. Peter touched the bell
Come in and choose your harp he cried
You've had your share of hell.

I. GOD

COMPETITION!

This kinda blows my brain apart, Lord. Is it wrong for me to ram my shoulder into a guy? to body-check him - hard? to slap away his best shot? Is it wrong, Lord is it?

When we were kids, I tackled my brother in a backyard game. Years smaller than he, I grabbed his ankle and rode him 30 yards before I tripped him — Thunk!. . .into the hard November ground. He looked across at me, surprised, "Way to go, kid," he grunted — and the rest of that day I was a tiger!

Couldn't competition be like that sometimes, Lord? Admiring the brother who outdoes you. . .but still fighting like crazy to win?

The Bible doesn't say much about sports. . .that was for the Greeks in those days - running naked, shocking Jews. But Paul must have known about the Olympics, 'cause he said to run the race - run it to win!

Lord, I know how Paul wanted me to compete; to fight my laziness, my selfishness, my desire to quit, my tendency to shove God into a corner, and run my life my way.

Competition grinds away my complacency, it polishes and lifts — lifts me to heights I didn't think possible. Competition demands my best, and that is of You.

I don't have to hate the guy who beats me — I can admire his ability, if God is in me. . .

Must I envy every time someone paints a great painting, or makes an A or hits a home run? Or can I rejoice in their art, their intelligence, their power? I am a child of God, unique, loved. I don't have to be what they are!

The Bible tells me "We are more than conquerors through Him who loved us." Your power, Lord, is that of a billion suns. Yet you live within me, telling me to love, even as I compete. Love People. Love You, as You love us, and died for us.

Help me take that to the ball field, Lord.

By Harold Myra

I. GOD

When God measures an athlete
he puts a tape around his Heart not his Waist.

* * *

A Sportsman's Prayer

Our Father,

As Jesus took the bread and broke it, took the cup of wine and poured it, so, also, He took the "Flesh" and wore it and played the game of life as a Christian sportsman.

Lord, help us to be good winners as well as losers in the game of life. Let us not pray to be the pitcher, or for any prominent place in the line-up. Play us anywhere you need us. We ask only that you give us the patience, courage and stamina to give You the best we've got in the game.

If we wind up as the catcher, and many bad hops, wild pitches and foul tips come our way, may we not complain, nor alibi, nor protest that the game was a frame-up. Let us never side-step one that is too hot to handle.

Lord, if we turn out to be the hitting star, keep us humble in heart.

Please play us wherever You will in such a way that You will have no regrets for having given us the chance.

And finally, dear Lord, when we reach that "last big inning" and the evening shadows are falling across home plate may we not have to "slide in" nor be "squeezed in." But grant that we will get that last big hit and trot safely home.

C. Wesley Grisham

* * *

To Sportsmen Who Love The Game

To sportsmen who love the game beyond all profit and fame.
I lift my glass. Here's to the creed of you, here's to the breed of you.
Here while the bugles call, here, where we rise and fall,
Here where we storm the wall, you paved the way.
Oh where the cannons roar, knowing the heart calls for,
You wrote the winning score, back in our day.

Grantland Rice

* * *

"There are no great men in this world, only great challenges which ordinary men rise to meet."

I. GOD

A COACH'S PRAYER

Help me to understand my players, their strengths and weaknesses, to treat them in such a way as to smooth their rough spots, and polish their strong traits. During this quest, O Lord, make me as demanding of myself as I am of them. Give me the courage to realize my mistakes and not knowingly commit them again.

May I not play a seriously injured boy. Forbid that I should laugh at their mistakes, to resort to sadism and ridicule as punishment. Let me not tempt a player to play dirty or illegal. So guide me game to game that I may demonstrate by all I say and do that maintaining training rules, hard work, and personal dedication are the ingredients of athletic success.

Reduce, I pray, vanity in me. May I cease to nag; and when we have lost, help me, O Lord, to hold my tongue.

Blind me to the small errors of my players and help me to see the good things that they do. Give me a ready word of honest praise.

Help me to treat my players as young men and not little boys; yet let me not expect of them the performance of adults. Let me not expect of them things that are impossible nor less of them than is possible. Guide me along those paths that will lead each player as close to his potential as is possible.

Forbid that I should ever punish them for falling short while trying their hardest. Grant that I may direct them to those experiences that will make of them better persons and have the courage always to withold experiences which I know will do them harm.

Make me so fair and just, considerate and understanding of my players that they may have genuine respect for me. Fit me to be the best example that is within me to be.

With all thy gifts, O God, give me poise, patience and humility.

* * *

Have faith in God —
Work harder than anyone else —
Be enthusiastic —

* * *

You tell me you're a Christian and I say, "What else did you get for your birthday? Show me!"

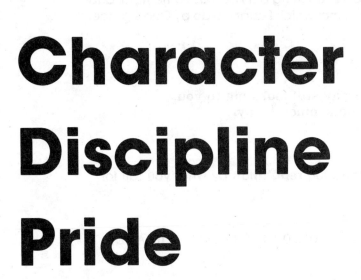

Winning Words

Chapter II

Character
Discipline
Pride

II. CHARACTER * DISCIPLINE * PRIDE

People are not **excellent** because they achieve great things; they achieve great things because they choose to be **excellent**.

* * *

1. **Prudence** — the ability to regulate and discipline one's self through the exercise of reason.
2. **Fortitude** — the endurance of physical or mental hardships or suffering without giving way under strain. It is: firmness of mind in meeting danger or adversity; resolute endurance; courage and staying power. It is the possesion of the stamina essential to face that which repels or frightens one, or to put up with the hardships of a job imposed. It implies triumph. Synonyms are grit, backbone, pluck, and guts.
3. **Temperance**— habitual moderation in the indulgence of appetites and passions.
4. **Justice**— the principle of rectitude and just dealing of men with each other; also conformity to it; integrity.
5. **Faith**— trust in God.
6. **Hope**— the desire with expectation of obtaining what is desired, or belief that it is obtainable.
7. **Charity**— the act of loving all men as brothers because they are sons of God. It stresses benevolence and goodwill in giving and in the broad understanding of others with kindly tolerance.

* * *

DON'T LOOK FOR MIRACLES. YOU ARE A *MIRACLE*.

* * *

I am only one, but I am one. I can't do everything but I can do something, and that which I can do, I ought to do, and that which I ought to do by God's grace, I shall do. . .

* * *

If what you did yesterday still looks big to you,
you haven't done much today.

* * *

Character is made by what you stand for; **reputation** by what you fall for.

* * *

WOULD THE BOY YOU WERE BE PROUD OF THE MAN YOU ARE?

II. CHARACTER * DISCIPLINE * PRIDE

If you fail to teach your child respect for others,
you and not he are responsible for his actions.

* * *

Maturity
Maturity is the ability to base a judgement on the big picture. . . the long haul.
Maturity is the ability to stick with a project or situation until it is finished.
Maturity is the ability to face unpleasantness, frustration, discomfort and defeat without complaint or collapse.
Maturity is the ability to live up to your responsibilties and this means being dependable, keeping your word. The world is filled with people who can't be counted on. People who never seem to come through in the clutches. People who break promises.
Maturity is the ability to make a decision and stand by it. . .
Maturity is the ability to harness your abilities and energies.

* * *

DON'T LOOK FOR AN ANSWER TO YOUR PROBLEM;
LOOK FOR LOTS OF ANSWERS, THEN CHOOSE THE BEST ONE.

* * *

The time to have "second thoughts" is before you make decisions, not after.

* * *

You don't win football games on **optimism**. You win with **preparation**.
Monte Clark

Are you trying to make something for yourself or something of yourself?

* * *

Some men are bigger, faster, stronger and smarter than others — but not a single man has a corner on dreams, desire, or ambition.
Duffy Daugherty

II. CHARACTER * DISCIPLINE * PRIDE

HE WHO CANNOT FORGIVE,
DESTROYS THE BRIDGE OVER WHICH HE MAY ONE DAY NEED TO PASS.

* * *

Do *all* the good you *can* by *all* the means you *can* in *all* the ways you *can*,
in *all* the places you *can* at *all* the times you *can* to *all* the people you *can*
as long as you *can*. . .

* * *

THERE IS NO RIGHT WAY TO DO THE WRONG THING.

* * *

Silence is not always golden. . .sometimes it is just plain yellow.

* * *

It is better to keep your mouth shut and be thought a fool, than to open it and
remove all doubt.

* * *

Temper is what gets most of us in trouble.
Pride is what keeps us there.

* * *

To Any Athlete

There are little eyes upon you and they're watching night and day;
There are little ears that quickly take in every word you say;
There are little hands, all eager to do anything you do!
And a little boy who's dreaming of that day he'll be like you.
You're the little fellow's idol; your the wisest of the wise in his little mind about
you no suspicions ever rise; he believes in you fervently, holds all you say and
do, he will say and do it your way when he's grown up like you.
There's a wide-eyed little fellow, who believes you're always right, and his ears
are always open, and he watches day and night.
You are setting an example everyday in all you do, for the little boy who's
waiting to grow up to be like you.

II. CHARACTER * DISCIPLINE * PRIDE

A MAN NEVER DISCLOSES HIS OWN CHARACTER SO CLEARLY
AS WHEN HE DESCRIBES ANOTHER'S.

* * *

Failure to prepare certainly means preparing to **fail.**

John Wooden

* * *

I WOULD RATHER BE DISLIKED FOR WHAT I AM,
THAN TO BE LIKED FOR WHAT I AM NOT.

* * *

Better a day of strife than a century of sleep.

* * *

As in nature, as in art, so in grace; it is rough treatment that gives
souls, as well as stones, their luster. The more the diamond is cut the
brighter it sparkles; and in what seems hard dealing, there God has no
end in view but to perfect his people.

K.S. Guthrie

* * *

There is no *easy* way.

* * *

The Right Angle To Approach Any Problem Is The TRY Angle.

* * *

You never get a second *chance to make a good* first *impression.*

* * *

TO BE BORN A GENTLEMAN IS AN ACCIDENT: TO DIE ONE, AN ACHIEVEMENT.

* * *

Who gossips to you will gossip *of* you.

* * *

You can tell more about a person by what he says about others. . .
than you can by what others say about him.

* * *

DON'T BELITTLE . . . **BE BIG**

II. CHARACTER * DISCIPLINE * PRIDE

CHARACTER IS THE RESULT OF TWO THINGS: MENTAL ATTITUDE AND THE WAY
WE SPEND OUR TIME.

ELBERT HOGGARD

* * *

If you treat a person as he is, he will remain as he is.
If you treat him as though he were what he could be and should be,
he will become what he could and should be.

* * *

Swearing is a device for making ignorance audible!

Mel Johnson

* * *

THIS IS A FINAL TEST OF A GENTLEMAN: HIS RESPECT FOR THOSE
WHO CAN BE OF NO POSSIBLE SERVICE TO HIM.

PHELPS

* * *

You are the fellow that has to decide whether you'll do it or toss it aside.
You are the fellow who makes up your mind whether you'll lead or linger
behind — whether you'll try for the goal that's afar or be contented to stay
where you are. Take it or leave it. Here's something to do — just think it
over. It's all up to you! What do you wish? To be known as a good man who's
willing to work, scorned for a loaner or praised by your chief, rich man or
poor man or beggar or thief? Eager or earnest or dull through the day, honest
or crooked? It's you who must say! You must decide in the face of the test
whether you'll shirk it or give it your best.

* * *

Talent will get you to the top but it takes character to keep you there.

John Wooden

* * *

Make your opponent *fear* and *respect* you.

Knute Rockne

* * *

Play for more than you can afford to lose, and you will learn the game.

II. CHARACTER * DISCIPLINE * PRIDE

If you don't take the time to find out what you're all about,
You'll never know what life is all about.

* * *

Dan Jesse to the NFCA:
"Keep football a tough sport that teaches men to think, to dare, to hit hard, to lead, to sacrifice, to fight, to win and to disdain the tie or the defeat.
College football is the greatest game man plays. Protect it well.
Keep it a tough sport and as a teacher of men.
Dare to hit hard, to lead, to sacrafice, to fight, to win, to disdain the tie or the defeat.
College football is the greatest game man plays.
Gentlemen. . .
PROTECT IT WELL.!

* * *

No price is too high to pay for a good reputation.

* * *

LET EVERYONE SWEEP IN FRONT OF HIS OWN DOOR
AND THE WHOLE WORLD WILL BE CLEAN.

* * *

Eat to live not live to eat.

* * *

THE BIGGER A MAN'S HEAD GETS, THE EASIER IT IS TO FILL HIS SHOES.

* * *

Pride. . .Character. . .Work Habits. . .Lead to success.

Rick Comley

* * *

The measure of a man's real character is what he would do if he knew he never would be found out.

T.B. Macaulay

* * *

It is my belief that *discipline*, well-earned *pride* and a high-degree of *unselfishness* contribute to achieving a desirable morale...the most important element in a successful team.

John Majors

II. CHARACTER * DISCIPLINE * PRIDE

The great thing in this world is not so much where we are, but in what direction we are moving.

O.W. Holmes

* * *

The person who properly disciplines himself to do those things that he does not especially care to do, becomes successful.

Frank Leahy

* * *

Some fellows stay right in the rut while others head the throng.
All men may be born equal but — they don't stay that way long.
There is many a man with a gallant air, goes galloping to the fray;
But the valuable man is the man who's there when the smoke has cleared away.
Some "don't get nuthin' out of life" but when their whines begin,
We often can remind them that they "don't put nuthin' in."

* * *

IT IS MORE IMPORTANT TO KNOW WHERE YOU ARE GOING THAN TO GET THERE QUICKLY.

M. Newcomber

The Measure of a Man

NOT — How did he die?
BUT — How did he live?
NOT — What did he gain?
BUT — What did he give?
These are the units to measure the worth of a man,
as a man, regardless of birth.

* * *

Before you flare up at anyone's faults, take time to count ten, TEN OF YOUR OWN.

* * *

Character is a conquest, *not a bequest.*

II. CHARACTER * DISCIPLINE * PRIDE

The guy who gets ahead, is the guy who does more than is necessary
— and keeps on doing it.

* * *

Men are born with two eyes and one tongue,
in order that they should see twice as much as they say.

C.C. Cocton

* * *

Resolutions

No one will get out of this world alive. Resolve therefore in the year to maintain a sense of values.

Take care of yourself. Good health is everyone's major source of wealth.

Without it, happiness is almost impossible. Resolve to be cheerful and helpful. Avoid angry, abrasive persons. They are generally vengeful. Avoid zealots. They are generally humorless. Resolve to listen more and talk less. No one ever learns anything by talking. Be leary of giving advice. Wise men don't need it, and fools won't heed it.

Resolve to be tender with the young, compassionate with the aged, sympathetic with the striving and tolerant of the weak and the wrong.

Sometimes in life you will have been all of these. Do not equate money with success. There are many successful money-makers who are miserable failures as human beings. What counts most about success is how a man achieves it.

Resolve to love, next year, someone you didn't love this year. Love is the most enriching ingredient of life.

* * *

"GREATNESS Cannot be achieved without DISCIPLINE."

* * *

When a man is wrapped up in himself, he makes a pretty small package.

* * *

CHARACTER IS WHAT A MAN IS IN THE DARK

II. CHARACTER * DISCIPLINE * PRIDE

THREE KINDS OF ATHLETES

On all squads there are three kinds of athletes.

First, there is the athlete who is a help. He is the one who takes a keen interest in the whole concern. He feels that he is a part of the set-up, and takes pride in it. Every now and then he suggests some improvement. Often he does more than he is expected to do. When he is given a job to do, he does not enlarge on the difficulties or the responsibility of it. He just pitches in and does it.

Secondly, there is the athlete who is a habit. He is a good worker. He takes an interest, more or less, in his job, but seldom concerns himself in the least about the whole concern. He has learned to do one thing, and does it reasonably well. His work is all a matter of habit. He hates to be shifted from one job to another. He lacks drive. He is a good man, but he has nailed himself down to a routine, and sees anything outside that routine as a nuisance rather than an opportunity.

The third type of athlete is a hindrance. He is the one who dislikes his job. He does not want to work, and he almost feels a grievance against anyone who gives him a chance to better his lot. He never has a good word for anyone or anything. He is strong on objecting, great on refusing, marvelous on criticizing, but weak on doing. He is against everything that spells an effort. He can't take it. He never takes correction in good spirit; instead, he walks off with a growl. He is an athlete who can never be promoted or advanced. He is a hindrance.

* * *

The Substitute

To fate resigned, he waits upon the bench
and leans his chin upon his hands.

He watches every play and vaguely hears
the cheers that thunder from the stands.

Out there his teammates execute the plays
his sweat and toil helped them to learn,

While he, a sub, can only watch and hope
and patiently await his turn.

The din of cheering crowds rolls o'er his head.
Unknown, the service he performs.

They only see him waiting for his chance,
the chance that often never comes.

Unsung, but still alert to give his best,
Content when thousands laud his mates;

Successful teams were never built without
The Sub, who hopes and works and waits.

II. CHARACTER * DISCIPLINE * PRIDE

"Don't Count The Days, Make The Days Count."

* * *

If I Had A Boy

If I had a boy, I would say this to him, Son, be fair and be square in the race you must run, be brave if you lose and meek if you win; be better and nobler than I've been; be honest and fearless in all that you do, and honor the name I have given you.

If I had a boy, I would want him to know, we reap in this life just about as we sow; and we get what we earn, be it little or great, regardless of luck and regardless of fate. I would teach him and show him the best that I could, that it pays to be honest and upright and good.

Frank Carleton Nelson

* * *

The real measure of an athlete is not what he is. . . but what he could be.

* * *

PLAYIN' SQUARE

Don't count the game as lost, my boy,
because the runs are more
for the opposing team than yours.
What matter is the score?
Why, being beaten can't impair
your courage when you're playin' square.

When bigger game and bigger stakes
are yours to lose and win,
don't waste your time connivin' for
advantage — just dig in.
And do your best to claim your share;
But first be sure you're playin' square.

Jos. R. Cushing

* * *

So LIVE that you wouldn't be ashamed to sell the family parrot to the town gossip.

Will Rogers

Inability to tell good from evil is the greatest worry of a man's life.

Cicero

II. CHARACTER * DISCIPLINE * PRIDE

The people most preoccupied with titles and status
are usually the least deserving of them.

* * *

WE NEED MEN

. . .who cannot be bought. . .whose word is their bond.

. . .who put character above wealth. . .who possess opinions and a will.

. . .who are larger than their vocations.

. . .who do not hesitate to take chances.

. . .who will make no compromise with wrong.

. . .who will not lose their individuality in a crowd.

. . .who will be as honest in small things as in great things.

. . .who will not say they do it "because everybody else does it.

. . .whose ambitions are not confined to their own selfish desires.

. . .who give thirty-six inches to the yard and thirty-two quarts to the bushel.

. . .who will not have one brand of honesty for business purposes and another for private life.

. . .who are true to their friends through good report and evil report, in adversity as well as in prosperity.

. . .who do not believe that shrewdness, sharpness, cunning and long-headedness are the best qualities for winning success.

. . .who are not ashamed or afraid to stand for the truth when it is unpopular, who can say "no" with emphasis, although all the rest of the world says "yes."

California Free Enterprise Association

* * *

DISCIPLINE IS THE REFINING FIRE
BY WHICH TALENT BECOMES ABILITY.

Roy Smith

* * *

Character is much easier kept than recovered.

* * *

REPUTATION IS WHAT MEN THINK YOU ARE:
CHARACTER IS WHAT GOD KNOWS YOU ARE.

* * *

Only a Mediocre Person Is Always At His Best.
Somerset Maugham

II. CHARACTER * DISCIPLINE * PRIDE

You are today where your thoughts have brought you.
You will be tomorrow where your thoughts take you.

James Allen

* * *

The man who is bigger than his job keeps his cool. He does not lose his head, he refuses to become rattled, to fly off in a temper. The man who would control others must be able to control himself. There is something admirable, something inspiring, something soul-stirring about a man who displays coolness and courage under extremely trying circumstances. A good temper is not only a business asset, it is the secret of health. The longer you live, the more you will learn that a disordered temper breeds a disordered body.

B.C. Forbes

* * *

THE TRUE PERFECTION OF MAN LIES NOT IN WHAT MAN HAS,
BUT IN WHAT MAN IS.

Oscar Wilde

* * *

How Did You Play?

How did you play when the game was on,
When the odds were great and hope was gone,
When the enemy team, with aim so true,
Was dragging the victory away from you?
When strength and speed and endurance quit,
Did honor keep pace with determined grit.
Did you keep the faith with the rules of the game?
Did you play up square without fear or shame?
Did your smile of cheer make the team your friend,
As you fought it through to the bitter end?
Did your self-respect rise a notch or two?
Are you a bigger MAN now the game is through?

William Ralph LaPorte

* * *

A man's reputation is the opinion people have of him,
his character is what he really is.

Jack Miner

II. CHARACTER * DISCIPLINE * PRIDE

"A CHAMPION MUST HAVE THE DESIRE FOR PERFECTION,
AND THE WILL TO PUNISH HIMSELF IN THE PROCESS."

* * *

The Bench Warmer

The radio screams and the papers print reams
for the player who carries the ball,
While never a word is written or heard of
the players who sit through it all.
But there on the bench a dozen hearts wrench
when a man goes in the fray.
They never go in, but they take it and grin—
for them it's all work and no play.
When the vacant seats stare you will find them
all there in the thick of the strife and the storm.
They are battered and bruised — it's for practice
they're used in the game they just keep the bench warm.
So take off your hat to the players who sat
through the Saturday afternoon game,
And remember that they had a part in the play
That to others brought glory and fame.

C.J. Perkins

* * *

"TRUE GREATNESS CONSISTS OF BEING GREAT IN LITTLE THINGS."

* * *

"One cannot always be a hero, one can always be a man."

* * *

From Roses to Raspberries

The lad they are cheering with accents endearing,
whose pathway is strewn with roses so red;
May boot one tomorrow and learn to his sorrow,
that raspberries grow when roses are dead.
So a word of advice to the popular star,
from roses to raspberries ain't very far.

* * *

"Courage is the same size in any man."

* * *

"THE TOUGHER THE JOB THE GREATER THE REWARD."

II. CHARACTER * DISCIPLINE * PRIDE

"The surest way not to fail, is to be determined to succeed."

* * *

What is Class?

Class never runs scared. It is sure footed and confident in the knowledge that you can meet life head on and handle whatever comes along.
Jacob had it. Esau didn't. Symbolically, we can look to Jacob's wrestling match with the angel. Those who have class have wrestled with their own personal "angel" and won a victory that marks them thereafter.
Class never makes excuses. It takes its lumps and learns from past mistakes.
Class is considerate of others. It knows that good manners is nothing more than a series of petty sacrifices.
Class bespeaks an aristocracy that has nothing to do with ancestors or money. The most affluent blueblood can be totally without class while the descendant of a Welsh miner may ooze class from every pore.
Class never tries to build itself up by tearing others down. Class is ALREADY up and need not strive to look better by making others look worse.
Class can "walk with kings and keep its virtue and talk with crowds and keep the common touch." Everyone is comfortable with the person who has class — because he is comfortable with himself.
If you have class you don't need much of anything else. If you don't have class, no matter what else you have — it doesn't make much difference.

* * *

You can't keep a good man down, or a bad man up.
P.K. Thomajan

* * *

"Hustle: You can't survive without it."

* * *

THE QUITTER GIVES AN ALIBI,
THE MONGREL, HE GETS BLUE
THE FIGHTER GOES DOWN FIGHTING,
BUT THE THOROUGHBRED COMES THRU.

II. CHARACTER * DISCIPLINE * PRIDE

"Winning isn't everything, but *wanting* to win is."

* * *

Maturity is the ability to tolerate an injustice without wanting to get even.

Maturity is patience. It is the willingness to postpone immediate gratification in favor of the long-term gain.

Maturity is perseverance, sweating out a project in the face of heavy opposition and discouraging setbacks.

Maturity is the capacity to face unpleasantness and frustration, discomfort and defeat without complaint, collapse or attempting to find someone to blame.

Maturity is humility. It is being big enough to say, "I was wrong." And when right, the mature person is able to forego the satisfaction of saying, "I told you so."

Maturity is the ability to evaluate a situation, make a decision and stick with it. The immature spend their lives exploring possibilities, changing their minds and in the end they do nothing.

Maturity means dependability, keeping one's word, coming through in a crisis. The immature are masters of the alibi. They are confused and disorganized. Their lives are a maze of broken promises, former friends, unfinished business and good intentions that never materialized.

Maturity is the art of living in peace with that which we cannot change, the courage to change that which can be changed and the wisdom to know the difference.

* * *

"ALWAYS REMEMBER — ANYTHING IS YOURS
IF YOU ARE WILLING TO — PAY THE PRICE."

* * *

If we would create something, we must be something.

* * *

Pass protection is a team proposition, and you must care about each other to the extent that you will sacrifice your own body to help a fellow lineman and protect your quarterback.

* * *

"Tell me how much you know of the sufferings of your fellow man,
and I will tell you how much you have loved them."

II. CHARACTER * DISCIPLINE * PRIDE

Be understanding to your enemies.
Be loyal to your friends.
Be strong enough to face the world each day.
Be weak enough to know you cannot do everything alone.
Be generous to those who need help.
Be frugal with what you need yourself.
Be wise enough to know that you do not know everything.
Be foolish enough to believe in miracles.
Be willing to share your joys.
Be willing to share the sorrow of others.
Be a leader when you see a path others have missed.
Be a follower when you are shrouded by the mists of uncertainty.
Be the first to congratulate an opponent who succeeds.
Be the last to criticize a colleague who fails.
Be sure where your next step will fall, so that you will not stumble.
Be sure of your final destination, in case you are going the wrong way.
Be loving to those who love you.

* * *

"ASSOCIATE YOURSELF WITH MEN OF GOOD QUALITY
IF YOU ESTEEM YOUR OWN REPUTATION:
FOR IT IS BETTER TO BE ALONE THAN IN BAD COMPANY."
George Washington

* * *

"Self respect cannot be hunted. It cannot be purchased. It is never for sale. It cannot be fabricated out of public relations. It comes to us when we are alone, in quiet moments, in quiet places, when we suddenly realize that, knowing the good, we have done it; knowing the beautiful, we have served it; knowing the truth, we have spoken it."

A. Witney Griswald

* * *

"GIVE ME A MAN WHO HOLDS ON WHEN OTHERS LET GO, WHO PUSHES AHEAD WHEN OTHERS TURN BACK, WHO STIFFENS UP WHEN OTHERS RETREAT, WHO KNOWS NO SUCH WORDS AS 'CAN'T' AND 'QUIT' AND I'LL SHOW YOU A MAN WHO WILL **WIN IN THE END.**

* * *

The totally dedicated and committed will hustle all the way and make the Game Breaker. This is a part of our total offense and defense and we must have it to WIN.

Winning Words

Chapter III

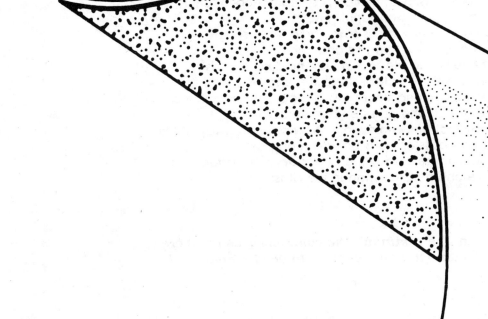

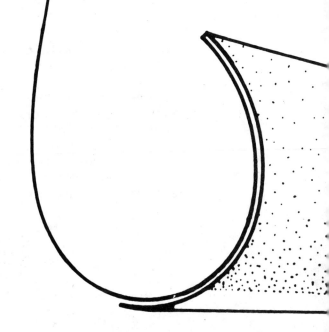

Courage

Leadership

III. COURAGE * LEADERSHIP

COURAGE is what it takes to stand up and speak;
COURAGE is also what it takes to sit down and listen.

* * *

THE MAN IN THE GLASS

When you get what you want in your struggle for self
  And the world makes you king for a day,
Just go to the mirror and look at yourself
  And see what that man has to say.
For it isn't your father, mother or wife
  Whose judgement upon you must pass;
The fellow whose verdict counts most in your life,
  Is the one staring back from the glass.
Some people may think you a straight-shootin' chum
  And call you a wonderful guy,
But the man in the glass says you're only a bum —
  If you can't look him straight in the eye.
He's the fellow to please—never mind all the rest,
  For he's with you clear up to the end.
And you've passed your most dangerous, difficult test
  If the man in the glass is your friend.
You may fool the whole world down the pathway of life
  And gets pats on your back as you pass.
BUT your final reward will be heartaches and tears—
If you've cheated the man in the glass!

* * *

You can't be common. The common goes nowhere.
You must be uncommon to be champion.

* * *

MY CREED

By Dean Alfan

  I do not choose to be a common man. It is my right to be uncommon. . .
if I can. I seek opportunity — not security. I do not wish to be a kept citizen,
humbled and dulled by having the State look after me. I want to take the
calculated risk; to dream and to build, to fail and to succeed. I refuse to
barter incentive for a dole. I prefer the challenges of life to the guaranteed
existence; the thrill of fulfillment to the stale calm of Utopia. I will not trade
freedom for beneficence, nor my dignity for a handout. I will never cower
before any master or bend to any threat. It is my heritage to stand erect,
proud and unafraid; to think and act for myself, enjoy the benefits of my
creations, to face the world boldly and say: *"This is what I have done."*

III. COURAGE * LEADERSHIP

The Responsibilities of Sportsmanship

The Player. . .
1) Treats opponents with respect.
2) Plays hard, but plays within the rules.
3) Exercises self-control at all times, setting the example for others to follow.
4) Respects officials and accepts their decisions without gesture or argument.
5) Wins without boasting, loses without excuses, and never quits.
6) Always remembers that it is a privilege to represent the school and community.

The Coach. . .
1) Treats own players, and opponents, with respect.
2) Inspires in the athletes a love for the game and the desire to compete fairly.
3) Is the type of person he/she wants the athletes to be.
4) Disciplines those on the team who display unsportsmanlike behavior.
5) Respects the judgement and interpretation of the rules by the officials.
6) Knows he/she is a teacher, and understands the athletic arena is a classroom.

The Official. . .
1) Knows the rules
2) Places welfare of the participants above all other considerations.
3) Treats players and coaches courteously and demands the same from them.
4) Works cooperatively with fellow officials, timers and/or scorers for an efficient contest.
5) Is fair and firm in all decisions, never compensating for a previous mistake.
6) Maintains confidence, poise and self-control from start to finish.

The Spectator. . .
1) Attempts to understand and be informed of the playing rules.
2) Appreciates a good play no matter who makes it.
3) Cooperates with and responds enthusiastically to cheerleaders.
4) Shows compassion for an injured player; applauds positive performances; does not heckle, jeer or distract players; and avoids use of profane and obnoxious language and behavior.
5) Respects the judgement and strategy of the coach, and does not criticize players or coaches for loss of a game.
6) Respects property of others and authority of those who administer the competition.
7) Censures those whose behavior is unbecoming.

III. COURAGE * LEADERSHIP

Conservative coaches have one thing in common: they are unemployed.
Chuck Knox

* * *

THERE ARE A FEW LEFT

Who put the game above the score,
Who rate the battle as the test,
Who stand content, amid the roar,
Where they have given out their best;
No matter what the prize at stake,
Who prove that they can give—and take.

Who have no fear of some defeat,
No vain regrets to haunt their night,
Because the race went to the fleet,
Because the stronger won the fight;
Who do their stuff—win, lose or draw,
And laugh at fate's inconstant law.
Grantland Rice

* * *

IT IS NOT THE CRITIC WHO COUNTS,
NOR THE MAN WHO POINTS OUT HOW THE STRONG MAN STUMBLED,
OR WHERE THE DOER OF DEEDS COULD HAVE DONE THEM BETTER.

* * *

Upon the fields of friendly strife are sown the seeds that, upon other fields, on other days, will bear the fruits of victory.
Gen. Douglas MacArthur

* * *

We are all alike; we have eyes, ears, arms, legs, and a head.
The difference is in the *heart*.

* * *

A person cannot teach what he does not know or lead where he does not go.

* * *

PROGRESS COMES FROM THE INTELLIGENT USE OF EXPERIENCE.

III. COURAGE * LEADERSHIP

Never put your finger on someone's faults
unless it's part of a helping hand.

* * *

Paradoxical Commandments of Leadership

1. People are illogical, unreasonable, and self-centered. Love them anyway.
2. If you do good, people will acuse you of selfish ulterior motives. Do good anyway.
3. If you are successful, you win false friends and true enemies. Succeed anyway.
4. The good you do today will be forgotten tomorrow. Do good anyway.
5. Honesty and frankness make you vulnerable. Be honest and frank anyway.
6. The biggest men with the biggest ideas can be shot down by the smallest men with the smallest ideas. Think big anyway.
7. People favor underdogs but follow only top dogs. Fight for a few underdogs anyway.
8. What you spend years building may be destroyed overnight. Build anyway.
9. People really need help but may attack you if you help them. Help them anyway.
10. Give the world the best you have and you'll get kicked in the teeth. Give the world the best you have anyway.

* * *

Only the small at heart are ashamed of doing small things and filling small assignments. The truly secure, self-confident person has no fears and shares a trait with history's greatest leaders — humility.

* * *

WHEN YOU ASK SOMEONE TO DO A JOB,
FIRST BE SURE IN YOUR MIND WHAT IT IS YOU WANT.

* * *

A leader is best when people barely know he exists. . . When his work is done, his aim fulfilled, they will say, "We did this ourselves."

* * *

Courage consists not in blindly overlooking danger,
but in seeing it and conquering.

III. COURAGE * LEADERSHIP

It's been said football is a contact sport. Not so! Football is a collision sport:
Dancing is a contact sport.

Duffy Daugherty

* * *

A good team leader is someone who takes a little more than his share
of the blame and a little less than his share of the credit.

* * *

Don't be afraid to take a big step if one is indicated.
You can't cross a chasm in two small jumps.

* * *

Leaders have two important characteristics: first they are going somewhere;
second they are able to persuade other people to go with them. . . .

* * *

Good Leaders Were First Great Followers.

* * *

Fatigue makes cowards of us all. . .
Vince Lombardi

* * *

HAVE IDEALS AND LIVE WITH THEM. . .

* * *

You have to have courage to make a decision and stick with it knowing that
people are going to criticize you no matter what you do.

* * *

No one can make you feel inferior without your consent.

* * *

The difference between the wise man and the fool?
The fool says what he knows — the wise man knows what he says.

* * *

Common sense is really not all that common.

III. COURAGE * LEADERSHIP

Courage is fear that has said its prayers. . .

* * *

Fat Cats Don't Fight. . .

* * *

President Ford To NFCA, 1975:

The football coach has a lonely job, he rarely gets much credit. And if he hears a kindly word. . .this is the group that said it.
He labors hard to build the sport, in a manner almost stately. But the only question he's ever asked is: "What have you won for us lately?"

And so you coaches, hear my wish: And don't sink into lethargy. Have some fun — there are a lot worse things than being burned in effigy!

* * *

EVERYTHING IS EASIER SAID THAN DONE.

* * *

When success turns an athlete's head, he faces failure.

* * *

About all there is to success is making promises and keeping them. . .

* * *

There is no scrap in scrapbooks.

* * *

Courage is the first of human qualities because it is the quality which guarantees all others.

W. Churchill

* * *

MUD THROWN IS GROUND LOST.

* * *

Good leaders learn to share decisions with others even though they alone must accept responsibility for the results.

III. COURAGE * LEADERSHIP

LEADERSHIP USUALLY BEGINS WITH A VISION OF SUCCESS; A GLIMMERING INTUITION THAT SOLUTIONS TO PROBLEMS ARE POSSIBLE.

* * *

What Today Will Bring

This is the beginning of a new day. God has given me this day to use as I will. I can waste it or use it for good. What I do today is important, because I'm exchanging a day of my life for it.
When tomorrow comes this day will be gone forever, leaving in its place something I have traded for it.
I want it to be gain; not loss: Good, not evil: Success not failure:
In order that I shall not regret the price I paid for it because the future is just a whole string of nows.

* * *

A man who cannot lead and will not follow invariably obstructs.

* * *

"Fight on, my men," Sir Andrew says, "A little I'me hurt, but yett not slaine; I'le but lye down and bleede awhile, and then I'll rise and fight againe."

* * *

The credit belongs to the man who is actually in the arena; whose fate is marred by dust and sweat and blood; who errs and comes short again; who knows the great enthusiasms: the great devotions, and spends himself in a worthy cause; who at best knows in the end the triumph of high achievement; and who at the worst, if he fails, at least fails while daring greatly; so that his place shall never be with those cold and timid souls who know neither victory nor defeat.

T. Roosevelt

* * *

Nobody said life would be easy. . . .and you only make it tougher if you feel sorry for yourself.

Morley Fraser

* * *

Courage conquers all things.

III. COURAGE * LEADERSHIP

One Man Plus Courage Is A Majority

* * *

The Only Way To Win

It takes a little courage, and a little self-control
And some grim determination, if you want to reach your goal.
It takes some real striving, and a firm and stern-set chin,
No matter what the battle, if you really want to win.
There's no easy path to glory, there's no rosy road to fame,
Life, however, we may view it, is no simple parlor game.
But its prizes call for fighting, for endurance and for grit,
For a rugged disposition and a "don't-know-when-to-quit."
You must take a blow or give one, you must risk and you must lose;
And expect that in the struggle you will suffer from the bruise.
But you must not wince or faulter, if a fight you once begin;
Be a man and face the battle — that's the only way to win.

* * *

I tell my people you treat me fair, I'll treat you fair.
You tell me the truth. I'll tell you the truth.
You may hate my guts because you believe something I don't
but we'll both know where we stand.
                                            Bo Schembechler

* * *

He That Loses Money Loses Little:
He That Loses Health Loses Much:
But He That Lose Courage Loses All.

* * *

It's not the size of the dog in the fight. It's the size of the fight in the dog.

* * *

When the going gets tough, the tough get going.

Winning Words

Chapter IV

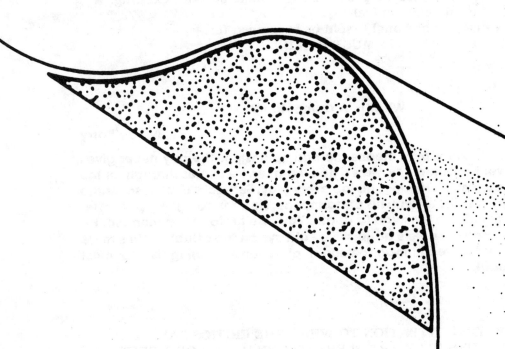

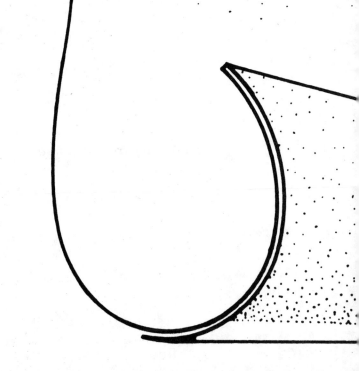

Dedication
Sacrifice
Desire

IV. DEDICATION * SACRIFICE * DESIRE

HE WHO WON'T BE DENIED WILL FIND A WAY.

* * *

MOTIVATE

MORALE - recognize individual - rewards, personal contact - dressing room.
OPPORTUNITY - getting it - convince with facts - film grade - stats.
TOGETHERNESS - dressing room unity - pictures - press guide - newspapers.
INITIATIVE - encourage to lead - find leaders early.
VARIETY - change off season program fun - make practice exciting.
ATTITUDE - how do players feel.
TRADITION - cannot be bought, sold or bargained for.
IT MUST BUILD. . .

* * *

What Is A Competitor?

By Ray Barry

He plays like every play means the championship. The guy never gives up. He's never beat mentally. He's a game player. He comes through for the team. He is consistent. He does his job every play. Setbacks don't discourage him. He's never satisfied with his performance. He keeps on going play after play - FULL SPEED. He runs you to death. You can't relax for a moment. He doesn't play cautious. He's aggressive - always on the attack. He's more interested in the team than personal glory and winning is the most important goal.

* * *

PAY NO ATTENTION TO WHAT THE CRITICS SAY.
A STATUE HAS NEVER BEEN ERECTED IN HONOR OF A CRITIC.
Jean Sibelius.

* * *

If hard work is the key to success, most people would rather pick the lock.
Claude McDonald

* * *

You cannot train a horse with shouts and expect it to obey a whisper.
Dagabert D. Runes

IV. DEDICATION * SACRIFICE * DESIRE

It is no disgrace to fail, but to lie there and grunt is.

* * *

TRY AND BE THE BEST

If you can't be the pine on top of the hill,
Be a scrub in the valley—but be
The best little scrub at the side of the hill;
Be a bush if you can't be a tree.

If you can't be a bush, be a bit of grass,
Some highway to happier make;
If you can't be a muskie; then just be a bass—
But the liveliest bass in the lake.

We can't all be captains, some have to be crew;
There's something for all of us here;
There's big work to do; there's lesser to do;
And the task we must do is near.

If you can't be a highway, then just be a trail,
If you can't be a sun, be a star.
It isn't by size that you win or you fail—
Be the *Best* of whatever you are.

Joe Dirk

* * *

CONDITION COMES FROM HARD WORK DURING PRACTICE AND PROPER MENTAL AND MORAL CONDUCT BETWEEN PRACTICES.

John Wooden

* * *

*I have never heard of anyone stumbling on something big
while sitting down.*

* * *

A FAULT RECOGNIZED IS HALF CORRECTED.

* * *

*It's amazing how much can be accomplished
if no one cares who gets the credit.*

* * *

Before strongly desiring anything,
we should look carefully into the
happiness of its owner.

La Rochefoucauld

IV. DEDICATION * SACRIFICE * DESIRE

YOU CAN'T HOOT WITH THE OWLS AT NIGHT
AND FLY WITH THE EAGLES DURING THE DAY.

* * *

It is not he that enters upon any career, or starts in any race, but he that runs well and perseveringly that gains the plaudits of others or the approval of his own conscience.

Alexander Campbell

* * *

NEVER BE SATISFIED

* * *

Believe in Yourself

Believe in yourself! Believe you were made to do any task without calling for aid.
Believe, without growing too scornfully proud, that you, as the greatest and least are endowed.
A mind to do thinking, two hands and two eyes are all the equipment God gives to the wise.
Believe in yourself! You're divinely designed and perfectly made for the work of mankind.
This truth you must cling to through danger and pain; the heights man has reached you can also attain. Believe to the very last hour, for it's true, That whatever you will you've been gifted to do.
Believe in yourself and step out unafraid.
By misgivings and doubt be not easily swayed.
You've the right to succeed; the precision of skill which betokens the great you can earn if you will!
The wisdom of ages is yours if you'll read.
But you've got to believe in yourself to succeed.

* * *

Counting time is not so important as making time count.

* * *

Fire your gun, then get ready to fire again,
instead of talking about the first shot.

IV. DEDICATION * SACRIFICE * DESIRE

FOOTBALL is a game that separates the men from the boys.
But also, it's a game that makes kids of us all.

Clettus Atkinson

* * *

I'm Gonna Try

I'm gonna try to play the game, and play it hard and play it fair.
I may not always meet the test as well as some more clever "guy,"
But while my heart beats in my chest, I'm gonna try.
I'm gonna try to stand the gaff, yet keep my nerve;
I'm gonna seek to love and work and play and laugh, never show
no yellow streak.
I'm gonna struggle to be kind and not grow hard of face and eye.
I'll flop at times, but never mind, I'm gonna try.
I'm gonna try to be a friend that folks can trust and who they know
Will be the same to the end, whether the luck runs high or low.
I'll hitch my wagon to a star, and set my goal up in the sky.
And though I may not get far, *I'm gonna try*.

* * *

Love your enemies; it will drive them crazy.

* * *

THE WORD AMERICAN ENDS IN — I CAN!

* * *

There are three kinds of people in the world. . .
The wills, the wants and the can'ts
The first accomplish everything;
The second oppose everything;
The third fail in everything.

* * *

There is a big difference between wanting to and willing to.

* * *

Football games are generally won by the boys with the greatest desire.

Bear Bryant

IV. DEDICATION * SACRIFICE * DESIRE

Happy is the person who can laugh at himself.
He will never cease to be amused.

Habib Bourguiba

* * *

I asked of life:
    "What have you to offer me?"
And the answer came:
    "What have you to give?"

* * *

A nation is strong or weak, it thrives or perishes upon what it believes to be true. If our youth is rightly instructed in the faith of our fathers; in the traditions of our country; in the dignity of each individual man, then our power will be stronger than any weapon of destruction that man can devise!"

Herbert Hoover

* * *

To Achieve All That Is Possible We Must Attempt The Impossible.

* * *

If you can imagine it, you can achieve it.
If you can dream it, you can become it.

* * *

THE BIGGEST SIN IN LIFE IS WASTING TIME

* * *

"Freedom is like a coin. It has the word privilege on one side and responsibility on the other. It does not have privilege on both sides. There are too many today who want everything involved in privilege but many refuse to accept anything that approaches the sense of responsibility.

Joseph R. Sizoo

* * *

Any criticism I make of anyone on my team,
I make because they are not performing to their full potential.

Vince Lombardi

IV. DEDICATION * SACRIFICE * DESIRE

THE IMPORTANT THING IS THIS, TO BE ABLE AT ANY MOMENT
TO SACRIFICE WHAT WE ARE FOR WHAT WE COULD BECOME.

Duboise

* * *

It Can Be Done

Somebody said that it couldn't be done, but with a chuckle replied, that "maybe it couldn't" but he would be one who wouldn't say so till he'd tried. So he buckled right in with the trace of a grin on his face. If he worried, he hid it. He started to sing as he tackled the thing that couldn't be done. And he did it. Somebody scoffed: "Oh, you'll never do that, at least no one has ever done it." So he took off his coat and took off his hat and the first thing he knew he'd begun it. With the lift of his chin and a bit of a grin, if any doubt rose he forbid it. He started to sing as he tackled the thing that couldn't be done, and he did it. There are thousands to tell you it cannot be done, there are thousands who prophesy failure; there are thousands to point out to you, one by one, the dangers that wait to assail you, but just buckle right in with a bit of a grin, then take off your coat and hat and go to it. Just start to sing as you tackle the thing that cannot be done and you'll do it.

* * *

There is only one method of meeting life's test:
Just keep on a-striving an' hope for the best.

* * *

Boosters

"I had a little hammer once
with which I used to strike
And I went knocking everywhere
At folks I didn't like.

I knocked most everybody
But I found it didn't pay
For when folks saw me coming
They went the other way.

I've thrown away my hammer, now,
As far as I could shoot,
And taken up a booster horn
And you should hear it toot.

I'm glad I'm with the boosters, now,
I like the way they do.
If you'll throw away your hammer,
I'll get a horn for you!"

IV. DEDICATION * SACRIFICE * DESIRE

WE MUST BE AGGRESSIVE FOR WHAT IS RIGHT
IF OUR WAY OF LIFE IS TO BE SAVED
FROM THOSE WHO ARE AGGRESSIVE FOR WHAT IS WRONG.

* * *

The Never-Say-Die Spirit

The sandlot Midgets
Played the Gas House Bears;
The football was patched and worn,
The field was littered
With tin cans and snares
And clothing was muddy and torn.

Faces were dirty;
The game nearly thru
Shirttails and pant seats were out.
A dozen loose teeth
And a black eye or two
Proved the Midgets had suffered a rout.

The Bears had a score
Of a hundred and two;
The Midgets had yet to score;
The big Midget center
Told his captain, "I'm Through'
We can't win—I won't play anymore."

The valiant Captain
Strutted his stuff;
Cited cases, by-laws and tenets;
Says he, "I'll admit that
It looks kinda tough
But an'thing c'n happ'n in two minutes."

Hist'ry sayeth not
how that game came out;
We assume the Gas Houses won it
But if that Captain's in school,
We've no doubt
They've a whale of a team
And he's on it.

H.V. Porter

* * *

Freedom must be constantly won and re-won.
It cannot survive unless those who cherish freedom
are prepared to nourish, live by, defend and develop it.

* * *

*A capable man on earth is more valuable
than any precious deposit under the earth.*

IV. DEDICATION * SACRIFICE * DESIRE

Everything cometh to him that waiteth,
so long as he who waiteth worketh like hell while he waiteth.

* * *

One Day At A Time

There are two days in every week about which we should not worry. . .
Two days which should be kept free from fear and apprehension. One of these days is yesterday, with its mistakes and cares, its faults and blunders, its aches and pains. Yesterday has passed forever beyond our control. All the money in the world cannot bring back yesterday. We cannot undo a single act we performed. We cannot erase a single word said. Yesterday is gone!
The other day we should not worry about is tomorrow, with its possible adversities, its burdens, its large promise and poor performance. Tomorrow is beyond our immediate control. Tomorrow's sun will rise, whether in splendor or behind a mask of clouds. But it will rise. Until it does we have no stake in tomorrow, for it is yet unborn.
This leaves only one day. . .today. Any man can fight the battles of just one day. It is when you and I add the burdens of two awful eternities - yesterday and tomorrow, that we break down.
It is not necessarily the experience of today that disturbs one's peace of mind. It is oftentime the bitterness for something which happened yesterday and the dread of what tomorrow may bring. Let us therefore live one day at a time.

* * *

Football requires a certain amount of Spartanism. It requires great sacrifice and self denial and you must have control of yourself.
Vince Lombardi

* * *

When you hurry in and out of the locker room
you hurry in and out of the big leagues.
Pee Wee Reese

* * *

Football is like life — it requires perseverance, self denial, hard work, sacrifice, dedication and respect for authority.

Vince Lombardi

IV. DEDICATION * SACRIFICE * DESIRE

The Time To Fight

My boy, when the fight is the grimmest
And it seems that you cannot gain
And you've hurtled yourself at the steel-like line
Again, and again and again.
And the tackle rebuffs your plunges
And the ends are as swift as light
And you've started to doubt your power,
Right then is the time to fight.

You feel that you're shot to pieces;
Ah, lad, but some day you'll know
That the battles of life and football
Are won by the final blow.
For the ones who have hit the hardest
Are as weakened, my boys, as you,
And the light must come down to courage,
The last vital drop or two.

So buck up your heart, old fellow,
And though all the heavens may fall,
Give 'em your heart-core wallop,
The weakest — yet best of all
And I'll tell you, dear boy, the heroes,
Who watch from their heights will say,
"There's a lad with the last punch courage;
MAKE WAY FOR A MAN, MAKE WAY. . .

* * *

**Some of us will do our jobs well and some will not,
but we will all be judged by only one thing — the result.**

* * *

SUCCESS DEMANDS SINGLENESS OF PURPOSE

* * *

Any criticism I make of anyone, I make only because he's a ballplayer not play-ing up to his potential. Any fine I levy on anyone, I levy because he's hurting not only himself but thirty-five other men.

* * *

Regardless of what you do put in, every game boils down to doing the things you do best, and doing them over and over again.

* * *

The amount that can be controlled and executed by a team
is controlled by the weakest man on it.

IV. DEDICATION * SACRIFICE * DESIRE

The difference between good and great
is just a little extra effort.

Duffy Daugherty

* * *

Until one is committed there is hesitancy, the chance to draw back, always ineffectiveness. Concerning all acts of initiative (and creation), there is one elementary truth, the ignorance of which kills countless ideas and splendid plans. That the moment one definitely commits oneself, then providence moves, too. All sorts of things occur to help one that would never otherwise have occurred.

William H. Murray

* * *

Concentrate on finding your goal, then concentrate on reaching it.

Col M. Friedsam

* * *

The Five "S's" That Are Necessary For Football
1. Spirit
2. Speed
3. Skill
4. Savvy
5. Size
(If you have the first four, don't worry about the fifth.)

* * *

"Every accomplishment great or small . . . starts with the decision. . .I'll Try!"

* * *

No horse gets anywhere till he is harnessed.
No stream ever drives anything until it is confined.
No life ever grows until it is focused, dedicated, and disciplined.

* * *

Fall down seven times, get up eight. . .

Winning Words

Chapter V

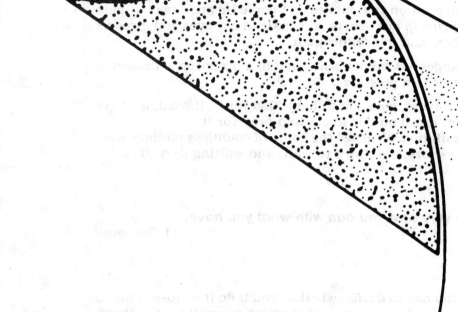

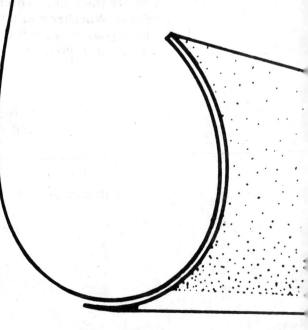

Enthusiasm
Ambition

V. ENTHUSIASM * AMBITION

**Size isn't everything. The whale is endangered,
while the ant continues to do just fine.**

* * *

Enthusiasm!

That certain something that makes us great - that pulls us out of the mediocre and commonplace - that builds into us Power. It glows and shines - it lights up our faces — Enthusiasm, the keynote that makes us sing and makes men sing with us.

Enthusiasm — the maker of friends, the maker of smiles, the producer of confidence. It cries to the world, "I've got what it takes." It tells all men that our job is a swell job, that the house we work for just suits us, the goods we have are the best.

Enthusiasm — the inspiration that makes us "Wake Up and Live." It puts spring in our step, spring in our hearts, a twinkle in our eyes and gives us confidence in ourselves and our fellow man.

Enthusiasm — it changes a dead pan salesman to a producer, a pessimist to an optimist, a loafer to a go-getter.

Enthusiasm — if we have it, we should thank God for it. If we don't have it, then we should get down on our knees and pray for it.
Upon the plains of hesitation, bleached the bones of countless millions who, on the threshold of victory, sat down to wait, and waiting they died.

* * *

Do the very best you can with what you have.

T. Roosevelt

* * *

You are the fellow who has to decide whether you'll do it or toss it aside. You are the fellow who makes up your mind whether you'll lead or linger behind. Whether you'll try for the goal that's afar or be contented to stay where you are. Take it or leave it. Here's something to do, just think it over it's all up to you.

* * *

Give the world the best you have
And the best will come back to you.

* * *

Enthusiasm without knowledge is like running in the dark.

V. ENTHUSIASM * AMBITION

**Some people are confident they could move mountains
if only somebody would just clear the foothills out of the way.**

* * *

Tomorrow Never Comes

Tomorrow comes — then it's today
    so if you have a debt to pay,
or work to finish; don't delay.
    Tomorrow never comes.

It's fatal to procrastinate,
    until you find it's just to late,
and then to put the blame on fate.
    Tomorrow never comes.

The putting right of some mistakes,
    the gesture that you meant to make,
The habit that you vowed to break.
    Tomorrow never comes.
So do it now—for fate can play
    some funny tricks; time slips away;
we cannot see beyond today.
    Tomorrow never comes.

* * *

You've got to have the goods, my boy, if you want to finish strong;
A bluff may work a little while, but not for very long;
A line of talk all by itself will seldom see you through;
You've got to have the goods, my boy, and nothing else will do.
The fight is pretty stiff, my boy, I'd call it rather tough;
And all along the routes are wrecks of those who tried to bluff;
They could not back their lines of talk to meet the final test,
You've got to have the goods, my boy, and that's no idle jest.

* * *

*The way to develop the best that is in a man is by appreciation and
encouragement.*

Charles Schwab

* * *

Enthusiasm in your work is half the battle won.

V. ENTHUSIASM * AMBITION

You will play as you practice.

* * *

In and Out

by Mary Sweeney

It's IN to care about your job; it's OUT to bite the hand that feeds you.

It's IN to be loyal to the company that pays you; it's OUT to breed discontent.

It's IN to give a little more than expected; it's OUT to split when you haven't finished the task at hand.

It's IN to be courteous - to anticipate the needs of fellow employees and plan accordingly; it's OUT to operate on your own, disregarding your obligation to others.

It's IN to appreciate all the benefits we enjoy; it's OUT to take all the benefits without making the best of what remains.

It's IN to praise fellow workers, while they're alive to hear it; it's OUT to wait until their wakes to say something nice.

It's IN to communicate with each other; it's OUT to withhold what is necessary to operate a business.

It's IN to contribute, to get involved, to remain active, it's OUT to be passive, and pessimistic and aloof.

It's IN to work and win; it's OUT to exist and lose.

It's IN to make productive the days that will never come back; it's OUT to let the days drift by and wonder why you died of boredom.

It's IN to love your job; it's OUT to endure it.

* * *

The right attitude and one arm
will beat the wrong attitude and two arms every time.

* * *

If you don't get everything you want,
think of the things you don't get that you don't want.

* * *

Ambition is an idol, on whose wing great minds are carried
only to extreme; to be sublimely great or to be nothing.

Sonthey

V. ENTHUSIASM * AMBITION

Even if you're on the right track, you'll get run over if you just sit there.

* * *

The Garden Of Life

First, plant five rows of P's
  Presence
  Promptness
  Preparation
  Perseverance
  Purity
Next, plant three rows of squash
  Squash gossip
  Squash indifference
  Squash unjust criticism
Then plant five rows of lettuce
  Let us be faithful to duty
  Let us be unselfish and loyal
  Let us obey the rules and regulations
  Let us be true to our obligations and
  Let us love one another
No garden is complete without turnups
  Turn up for meetings
  Turn up with a smile
  Turn up with determination to make
  everything counts for something good and
worthwhile.

* * *

The reason so many people are unhappy today and seeking help to cope with life is that they fail to understand what human existence is all about. Until we recognize that life is not just something to be enjoyed, but rather is a task that each of us is assigned we'll never find meaning in our lives and never truly be happy.

Dr. Victor Frankl
Holocaust Survivor

* * *

*The people most preoccupied with titles and status
are usually the least deserving of them.*

* * *

Neither you nor the world knows what you can do until you have tried
Ralph Waldo Emerson

V. ENTHUSIASM * AMBITION

If there's one thing we should let others find out for themselves, it's how great we are.

* * *

The Real Value of Football

The football field is one of the last sanctuaries of activity that is essentially and exclusively masculine. The basic elements of hard contact and physical competition provide the cornerstone around which the game is constructed. Left to themselves, the instinct for contact and competition would raise kmen scarcely above the level of the animal, but when their instincts are bounded by a strict code, a set of rules, we can see the human condition in microcosm.

Football then, provides a necessary outlet for the natural aggressiveness of men, while pointing to the equally natural need of rules, standards and ethical codes.

Mothers, try as you might, you will never fully understand the magnetic hold this game has over it's participants. You can never experience the feeling a football player has as he stands exhausted on a muddy field, bleeding and battered (perhaps in defeat but never defeated), wishing there was still another quarter to play. You will never know this feeling because this experience has been reserved for men — men who play football.

* * *

We accomplish in proportion to what we attempt.

* * *

Some fellows stay right in the rut while others head the throng.
All men may be born equal — but they don't stay that way long.
There is many a man with a gallant air, goes galloping to the fray;
But the valuable man is the man who's there when the smoke has cleared away.
Some say "I don't get nuthin' out of life" but when their whines begin,
We often can remind them that they "Don't put nuthin' in."

* * *

THREE OF THE MOST DIFFICULT THINGS IN LIFE ARE TO KEEP A SECRET, FORGET AN INJURY, AND MAKE GOOD USE OF LESIURE TIME.

V. ENTHUSIASM * AMBITION

The Saddest Words Of Tongue Or Pen
Are These Sad Words. . .it might have been.

* * *

Commitment to Excellence

"I owe most everything to football, in which I have spent the greater part of my life. I have never lost my respect, my admiration or my love for what I consider a great game. Each Sunday, after the battle, one group savours victory, another group lives in the bitterness of defeat. The many hurts seem a small price to have paid for having won, and there is no reason at all that is adequate for having lost. To the winner there is one hundred percent fun; and to the loser the only thing left for him is a one hundred percent resolution, one hundred percent determination.

It's a game, I think, a great deal like life in that it demands that a man's personal commitment be toward victory, even though you know that ultimate victory can never be completely won. Yet it must be pursued with all of ones might. Each week there's a new encounter, each year a new challenge. All of the rings and all of the money and all of the color and all of the display linger only in memory. The spirit, the will to win and the will to excel, these are the things that endure and these are the qualities that are so much more important than any of the events that occasion them. I would like to say that the quality of any man's life has got to be full measure of that man's personal commitment to excellence and to victory, regardless of what fields he may be in."

Vince Lombardi

* * *

YOU ONLY LIVE ONCE — IF YOU DO IT RIGHT ONCE IS ENOUGH.

* * *

There are few, if any, jobs in which ability alone is sufficient. Needed also are loyalty, sincerity, enthusiasm and cooperation.

* * *

Men do not stumble over mountains, but over molehills.
Confucius

* * *

The person who gets ahead is the one who does more
than is necessary and keeps on doing it.

V. ENTHUSIASM * AMBITION

A person who is enthusiastic soon has enthusiastic followers.

* * *

Try, Try Again

'Tis a lesson you should heed,
  Try, try again;
It at first you don't succeed
  Try, try again;
Then your courage should persevere,
  You will conquer, never fear;
  Try, try again.
Once or twice though you should fail,
  Try, try again;
If you would at last prevail,
  Try, try again;
If we strive, 'tis no disgrace
  Though we do not win each race;
What should you do in this case?
  Try, try again.
If you find your task is hard,
  Try, try again;
Time will bring you your reward,
  Try, try again;
All other folks can do,
  Why, with patience, should not you?
Only keep this rule in view,
  Try, try again!

from McGuffey's Reader

* * *

IF IT'S WORTH DOING AT ALL, IT'S WORTH DOING WELL.

* * *

He who would leap high must take a long run.
Danish Proverb

* * *

DO IT LIKE IT IS YOUR LAST CHANCE

* * *

Whatever you vividly imagine, ardently desire, sincerely believe,
and enthusiastically act upon. . .must inevitably come to pass.

* * *

Triumph is just the umph added to try!

V. ENTHUSIASM * AMBITION

Big Shots are usually Little Shots who kept on shooting.

* * *

Just for Today

Just for today I will live through the next 12 hours and not tackle my whole life problem at once.

Just for today I will improve my mind. I will learn something useful. I will read something that requires effort, thought and concentration.

Just for today, I will not find fault with a friend, relative or colleague. I will not try to change or improve anyone but myself.

Just for today I will have a program. I might not follow it exactly, but I will have it. I will save myself from two enemies—hurry and indecision.

Just for today I will exercise my character in three ways. I will do a good turn and keep it a secret.

If anyone finds out, it won't count.

Just for today I will do two things I don't want to do, just for the exercise.

Just for today I will be unafraid. Especially will I be unafraid to enjoy what is beautiful and believe that as I give to the world, the world will give to me.

Ann Landers
Nationally Syndicated Column
October 1972

* * *

To activate others, to get them to be enthusiastic,
you must first be enthusiastic yourself.

* * *

Good, Better, Best: Never let it rest,
till your Good is Better, and your Better is BEST.

* * *

There is no security in this life, only opportunity.

Gen. Douglas MacArthur

Winning Words

Chapter VI

Family

Friends

VI. FAMILY * FRIENDS

A FRIEND IS A PRESENT YOU GIVE YOURSELF.

* * *

THE FIFTIETH BOY

About one boy in fifty will remain after the feast and of his own accord offer to help clear the things up or to wash the dishes.

Do you know that Fiftieth Boy? There are forty-nine boys who are seeking jobs; the job seeks the Fiftieth Boy.

The Fiftieth Boy makes good the heart of his parents. The Fiftieth Boy smoothes the wrinkles out of his teacher's forehead, and takes the worry out of her mind. All the grouches and sour-faces brighten when they see the Fiftieth boy coming, for he is brave and cheery. The forty-nine "didn't think;" the Fiftieth Boy thinks. The Fiftieth Boy makes a confidant of his father.

He does not lie, steal, nor tattle, because he does not like to. When he sees a banana peel on the side-walk, where it is liable to cause some one to slip and fall, or a piece of glass in the road where it may puncture a tire, he picks it up. The forty-nine think it's none of their business.

The Fiftieth boy is a good sport. He does not whine when he loses. He does not sulk when another wins the prize. He does not cry when he is hurt. He is not afraid to do right nor ashamed to be decent. He looks you straight in the eye. He tells the truth, whether the consequences to him are unpleasant or not.

He is not a pig nor a sissy, but he stands up straight and is honest. He is pleasant and is not sorry for himself. He works as hard as he plays. Everybody is glad to see him. Do you have that kind of a boy at your house? If not, don't complain, there are not enough of them to go around.

* * *

WE DO NOT REMEMBER DAYS, WE REMEMBER MOMENTS.

* * *

The quality of a man's life is in direct proportion to his commitment to excellence, regardless of his chosen field of endeavor.

Vince Lombardi

* * *

The best way to better our lot is to do a lot better.

VI. FAMILY * FRIENDS

WHEN YOU HELP SOMEONE UP A HILL, YOU'LL FIND YOURSELF CLOSE TO THE TOP, TOO.

* * *

MY DAD
by Mamie Ozborn Odum

You have been a mighty dandy pal,
You held my baby hand,
You soothed away imagined hurts;
Helped me on my feet to stand.

You always knew each childish want,
And chased away my fears,
Encouraged me when things went wrong,
And wiped away my tears.

Yes, Dad, you walked each day with me.
When the pace was hard and long,
Undying courage you instilled,
Teaching right, condemning wrong.

You father — wisdom daily gave.
New courage to my heart,
Never tiring, just standing by,
Quietly doing your part.

When now we meet at manhood's gate,
You're the best pal I ever had,
You'll never know what you mean to me,
As I so simply say,
"THANKS, DAD!"

* * *

IF GOOD MEN WERE ONLY BETTER, WOULD WICKED MEN BE SO BAD?
J.W. Chadwick

* * *

Coming together is a **beginning;** keeping together is **progress;** working together is **success.**

Henry Ford

* * *

WHAT DO WE LIVE FOR, IF IT IS NOT TO MAKE LIFE LESS DIFFICULT FOR EACH OTHER?

George Eliot

* * *

It wouldn't be so bad to let one's mind go blank if one always remembered to turn off the sound. . .

VI. FAMILY * FRIENDS

If you want kids to improve, let them hear the
nice things you say about them.

* * *

If a child lives with criticism, *he learns to* condemn.
If a child lives with hostility, *he learns to* fight.
If a child lives with fears, *he learns to be* apprehensive.
If a child lives with pity, *he learns to feel* sorry *for himself.*
If a child lives with jealousy, *he learns to feel* guilty.
If a child lives with encouragement, *he learns to be* confident.
If a child lives with tolerance, *he learns to be* patient.
If a child lives with praise, *he learns to be* appreciative.
If a child lives with acceptance, *he learns to* love.
If a child lives with approval, *he learns to* like *himself.*
If a child lives with recognition, *he learns to have* a goal.
If a child lives with fairness, *he learns what* justice *is.*
If a child lives with honesty, *he learns what* truth *is.*
If a child lives with security, *he learns to have* faith *in himself and
in those about him.*
If a child lives with friendliness, *he learns that the world is a good
place in which to live.*

* * *

YOU CANNOT DO A KINDNESS TOO SOON FOR YOU NEVER KNOW
HOW SOON IT WILL BE TOO LATE.

* * *

A nod, a smile, you scarce believe how much the burden 'twill
relieve, thinking the world unfriendly.
A gracious work, a kindly deed, does more to help the human need
than any doctrine, form or creed.
So let's be friendly.

* * *

The time to make friends is before you need them.

* * *

BE KIND. REMEMBER EVERYONE YOU MEET IS FIGHTING A HARD BATTLE.

* * *

It's smart to pick your friends — but not to pieces.

VI. FAMILY * FRIENDS

MAKE NEW FRIENDS BUT KEEP THE OLD: THE FIRST ARE SILVER,
THE LATTER GOLD.

* * *

THE TEN COMMANDMENTS OF HUMAN RELATIONS

1. *Speak to people. There's nothing as nice as a cheerful greeting.*
2. *Smile at people. It takes 72 muscles to frown and only 14 to smile.*
3. *Call people by their name. The sweetest music to the ears is one's own name.*
4. *Be friendly and helpful. If you would have friends, be friendly.*
5. *Be cordial. Speak and act as if everything you did were a pleasure.*
6. *Be genuinely interested in people.*
7. *Be generous with praise, cautious with criticism.*
8. *Be considerate with the feelings of others; it will be appreciated.*
9. *Be thoughtful of others opinions. There are three sides to every controversy — yours, the others — and the right one.*
10. *Be alert to give service. What counts a great deal in life is what we do for others.*

* * *

Man is that foolish creature who tries to get even with
his **enemies** — and ahead of his **friends.**

* * *

NO PERSON STANDS SO TALL AS WHEN THEY STOOP TO HELP A
CHILD.

* * *

If I thought that a word of mine perhaps unkind and untrue,
would leave its trace on a loved one's face, I'd never speak it —
would you?

If I thought that a smile of mine might linger the whole day through
and lighten some heart with a heavier part, I'd not withhold it —
would you?

* * *

True friendship is like sound health, the value of it
is seldom known until it is lost.
C.C. Colton

* * *

WE'RE ALL IN THIS TOGETHER.

VI. FAMILY * FRIENDS

PEOPLE ARE LIKE SOUP —
THERE ARE TWO KINDS: **THICK** AND **THIN**.

* * *

THANK YOU MY FRIEND

I thank you for the many times you get in touch with me and all your contributions to my happy memory. I thank you for the friendly smile with which you always greet me and for the kind and thoughtful and the gracious way you treat me. You are the shining symbol of a friendship really true; and an inspiration wonderful in all I try to do. You are a soothing comfort to my very smallest sorrow and you instill the hope I need for every new tomorrow. and so I thank you for the joys and favors you extend and pray that God will bless you always my dear and faithful friend.

* * *

THE PRAYER OF A PARENT

Build me a son, O Lord, who will be strong enough to know when he is weak, and brave enough to face himself when he is afraid. One who will be

proud and unbending in defeat, but humble and gentle in victory. A son who will know that to know himself is the foundation stone of all true knowledge.

Rear him, I pray, not in the paths of ease and comfort, but under the stress and spur of difficulties and challenges. Here let him learn to stand up in the storm, here let him learn compassion for those who fail. Build me a son who will master himself before he seeks to master other men. Build me a son whose heart will be clean, whose goal will be high, one who will learn to laugh, yet never forget how to weep. One who will reach into the future, yet never forget the past. And after all these are his, add, I pray, enough of a sense of humor so that he may always be serious, yet never take himself too seriously. A touch of humility so that he may always remember the simplicity of true greatness, the open mind of true wisdom, the meekness of true wisdom, the meekness of true strength, Then, I will dare in the sacred recesses of my own heart, to whisper "I have not lived in vain!"

* * *

**There are three kinds of friends: best friends
guest friends
pest friends**

* * *

KEEP FRIENDSHIPS IN CONSTANT REPAIR . . .

VI. FAMILY * FRIENDS

YOU CAN GET ANYTHING IN THIS WORLD YOU WANT IF YOU
HELP ENOUGH PEOPLE GET WHAT THEY WANT.

* * *

IT IS NOT EASY
To apologize,
To begin over,
To be unselfish,
To take advice,
To admit an error,
To face a sneer,
To be charitable,
To keep on trying,
To be considerate,
To avoid mistakes,
To endure success,
To profit by mistakes,
To forgive and forget,
To think and then act,
To keep out of the rut,
To make the best of little,
To subdue an unruly temper,
To shoulder a deserved blame,
To recognize the silver lining—
But it always pays, try it!

* * *

THE ONLY WAY TO HAVE A TRUE FRIEND IS TO BE A TRUE FRIEND.

EMERSON

* * *

May the road rise to meet you,
May the wind be always at your back,
May the sun shine warm upon your face,
The rains fall soft upon your fields,
And until we meet again, may God
Hold you in the palm of His hand.

An Irish Blessing

* * *

IT IS CHANCE THAT MAKES BROTHERS
BUT HEARTS THAT MAKE FRIENDS.

* * *

Have respect for everyone and remember everyone is different.

VI. FAMILY * FRIENDS

Horse sense is what stops a horse from betting on people.

* * *

PLAYER'S CODE

- *Play the game for the game's sake*
- *Be generous when you win*
- *Be graceful when you lose*
- *Be fair always no matter what the cost*
- *Obey the laws of the game*
- *Work for the good of your team*
- *Accept the decisions of the officials with good grace.*
- *Believe in the honesty of your opponents*
- *Conduct yourself with honor and dignity*

Honestly and wholeheartedly applaud the efforts of your teammates and your opponents. The game that this Association will support must provide opportunities for:

a. *Fun, enjoyment and many other recreational satisfactions.*
b. *Achievement, recognition and the pursuit of excellence relative to the skill potential, personal competitive goals and physio/psycho needs of the participants.*
c. *The development of physical, mental, social and emotional fitness.*

The type of game that The Association will not support nor tolerate is:

a. *That which brings the game into disrepute.*
b. *That which results in physical or mental violence.*
c. *That which is morally indefensible.*

* * *

TROUBLE IS A GREAT SIEVE THROUGH WHICH WE SIFT OUR AQUAINTANCES: THOSE WHO ARE TOO BIG TO PASS THROUGH ARE FRIENDS.

* * *

Our real task on Earth will be to love those we don't have to.

* * *

We are not only our brothers keeper; in countless large and small ways we are our brothers maker.

B. Overstreet

* * *

The only exercise some folks get is jumping to conclusions.

VI. FAMILY * FRIENDS

A CLOSED MIND IS USUALLY EMPTY . . .
BECAUSE IT WON'T ALLOW ANYTHING TO ENTER.

* * *

PARENT'S CODE

Parents should remember:

- *Children have more need of example than criticism.*
- *Make athletic participation for your child and others a positive experience.*
- *Attempt to relieve the pressure of competition, not to increase it. A child is easily affected by outside influences.*
- *Be kind to your child's coach and to officials. The coach is a volunteer giving of personal time and money to provide a recreational activity for your child. The coach is providing valuable community service often without reward other than the personal satisfaction of having served the community.*
- *The opponents are necessary friends. Without them your child could not participate.*
- *Applaud good plays by your team and by members of the opposing team.*

Between the exuberance of the winner and the disappointment of the loser we find a person called a referee. All of them follow the same creed to watch every move of every player and to call the game to the best of his/her ability.

- *Do not openly question his/her judgement and never the honesty.*
- *Accept the results of fair play, integrity and sportsmanship.*
- *Accept the results of each game. Encourage the child to:*
     a. Be gracious in victory, and
     b. Turn defeat to victory by working towards improvements.

Parental evaluation carries a great deal of weight with the pre-adolescent. The attitude shown by parents at games towards the child, the opposing team, the officials and the coach influence the child's values and behavior in sports.

* * *

HARDENING OF THE HEART AGES PEOPLE MORE QUICKLY
THAN HARDENING OF THE ARTERIES.

* * *

Be slow in choosing a friend, slower in changing.

VI. FAMILY * FRIENDS

TRUST IS THE GREATEST GIFT ONE PERSON CAN GIVE ANOTHER.

* * *

IN A FRIENDLY SORT OF WAY

by James Witcome Riley

When a man ain't got a cent and he's feeling kind of blue, and the clouds hang dark and heavy and won't let the sunshine through, it's a great thing, oh, my brethren, for a fellow just to lay his hand upon your shoulder in a friendly sort o'way.

It makes a man feel curious, it makes the teardrops start, an you sort o'feel a flutter in the region of your heart. You can't look up and meet his eyes, you just don't know what to say, when a hand is on your shoulder in a friendly sort o'way.

Oh, the world's a curious compound, with its honey and its gall, with its cares and bitter crosses, but a good world after all. And a good God must have made it-least-wise that is what I say, when a hand is on my shoulder in a friendly sort o'way.

* * *

JUST TELL HIM NOW

If with pleasure you are viewing any work a man is doing,
If you like him or you love him, tell him now;
Don't withhold your approbation till the parson makes oration,
And he lies with snowy lilies o'er his brow;
For no matter how you shout it, he won't really care about it,
He won't know how many teardrops you have shed.
If you think some praise is due him,
Now's the time to slip it to him,
For he cannot read his tombstone when he's dead.

More than fame and more than money,
Is the comment, kind and sunny,
And the hearty, warm approval of a friend;
For it gives to life a savor, makes you richer, stronger, braver—
Gives you heart and hope and courage to the end.
If he earns your praise, bestow it;
If you like him, let him know it;
Let the word of true encouragement be said.
Do not wait till life is over and he's underneath the clover,
For he cannot read his tombstone when he's dead.

VI. FAMILY * FRIENDS

Behind an able man there are always other able men.

* * *

"THE CHAMP"

"C"   conditioned for the task supreme
        confident in coach and team;
        courageous when the goin's rough,
        champions never say "enough."

"H"   heart to meet the game's bad breaks;
        head to know just what it takes;
        hands that work through thick and thin;
        honest champions play to win.

"A"   ambitions to develop now,
        abilities that God endows.
        aiming high to meet the test;
        a champion wants to be the best.

"M"   marked and watched where'er he goes;
        model traits he has to show.
        manliness, if in defeat;
        modest if in the victor's seat.

"P"   practice, practice ever on the move;
        plugging daily to improve.
        perfection? that he'll never see,
        peerless champions just try to BE.

                                        C.M. Cosh

* * *

TACT IS THE ART OF MAKING A POINT WITHOUT MAKING AN ENEMY.

* * *

Mistrust the man who finds everything good,
the man who finds everything evil, and still more,
the man who is indifferent to everything.

* * *

One of the mysteries of life is how the boy who wasn't good enough to marry the daughter can be the father of the smartest grandchild in the world.

* * *

I may not be easy to reach, but I may be worth it.

* * *

You'll never know how much I appreciate you,
because I'll probably never tell you.

VI. FAMILY * FRIENDS

Do unto others as if others were you.

* * *

WHEN IT COMES TO HELPING OTHERS, SOME PEOPLE STOP AT NOTHING.

* * *

*Love reduces **friction** to a **fraction**.*

* * *

TIME WOUNDS ALL HEELS.

* * *

A song's not a song til you sing it,
A bell's not a bell til you ring it,
Love in your heart wasn't put there to stay,
Love isn't love til you give it away.
Oscar Hammerstein

* * *

FRIENDSHIPS MULTIPLY JOYS AND DIVIDE GRIEFS.
H.G. BOHN

* * *

One moment of patience may ward off a great disaster;
one moment of impatience may ruin a whole life.

* * *

DON'T WALK IN FRONT OF ME, I MAY NOT FOLLOW.
DON'T WALK BEHIND ME, I MAY NOT LEAD.
BUT WALK BESIDE ME, AND BE MY FRIEND.

* * *

None goes his way alone. All that we send into the
lives of others comes back into our own.
Edwin Markham

* * *

ASSOCIATE WITH MEN OF GOOD QUALITY, IF YOU ESTEEM YOUR
OWN REPUTATION; FOR IT'S BETTER TO BE ALONE THAN IN BAD
COMPANY.

GEORGE WASHINGTON

* * *

Friendship is a silent gentleman that makes no parade.

VI. FAMILY * FRIENDS

A FRIEND IS SOMEONE WHO CAN SEE THROUGH YOU
AND STILL ENJOYS THE SHOW.

* * *

DAD

He is the creator. He is the builder, the teacher, the comedian, the repairman, the disciplinarian, and the chairman of the sounding board. He is the grouch, the warm, the cold, the soft, the hard, the gentle, the rough, the kind, the cruel, the man, the father . . . in his children's lives.

He has calloused hands and balding head. He has wrinkles that show when he smiles. He receives no anesthetic and when everyone cries, he dies inside because he is not supposed to show tears. He has a smell that only his children love. He goes someplace everyday called work. He comes home with a sack of doughnuts and feels he is carrying a bag of gold.

He is grouchy when he is tired and happy when he is rested. He smiles when he is scared. He frowns when he is joking. He hurts when his kids ache. He is never quite the man his son thinks he is and he is never quite the hero his daughter knows he is.

He listens to fears, doubts, joys and sorrows. He repairs broken dolls and flat bicycle tires. He mends crushed hopes and broken hearts. He rules in joy and empathizes in sorrow.

He creates dreams, plans and goals. He builds direction that evolves into purpose. He teaches senses of responsibility and he teaches honesty. This structure is his Michelangelo, his masterpiece. This masterpiece is what he lives for. He believes in it. He lives in this belief. He would die in this belief. This belief is the future for his gang. His gang is his life. His life is his gang.

* * *

COUNT YOUR LIFE BY SMILES NOT TEARS.
COUNT YOUR AGE BY FRIENDS NOT YEARS.

* * *

There is a destiny that makes us brothers, none goes his way alone. All that we send into the lives of others comes back into our own.

* * *

A GOOD COACH NEEDS A PATIENT WIFE, A LOYAL DOG AND A GREAT QUARTERBACK, BUT NOT NECESSARILY IN THAT ORDER.

BUD GRANT

Winning Words

Chapter VII

Losing
Quitting

VII. LOSING * QUITTING

TOO MANY FELLOWS THINK THEY CAN PUSH THEMSELVES FORWARD
BY PATTING THEMSELVES ON THE BACK.

* * *

DON'T QUIT

When things go wrong, as they sometimes will, when the road you're trudging seems all uphill, when the funds are low and the debts are high, and you want to smile but you have to sigh, when care is pressing you down a bit — rest if you must, but don't you quit.

Life is queer with its twists and turns. As everyone of us sometimes learns. And many a fellow turns about when he might have won had he stuck it out. Don't give up though the pace seems slow — you may succeed with another blow.

Often the goal is nearer than it seems to a faint and faltering man; often the struggler has given up when he might have captured the victor's cup; and he learned too late when the night came down, how close he was to the golden crown.

Success is failure turned inside out — the silver tint of the clouds of doubt, and when you never can tell how close you are, it may be near when it seems afar; so stick to the fight when you're hardest hit — it's when things seem worst, you musn't quit.

* * *

I'd rather see a lesson
than to hear one any day,
I'd rather you'd walk with me
than to merely show me the way.

The eye's a better teacher
and more willing than the ear,
and counsel is confusing
but examples always clear.

The best of all the teachers
are the ones who live the deeds,
to see the good in action
is what everybody needs.

I soon can learn to do it
if you let me see it done,
I can see your hand in action
but your tongue too fast may run.

And the counsel you are giving
may be very fine and true,
but I'd rather get my lesson
by observing what you do!

VII. LOSING * QUITTING

TOO MANY OF US CONDUCT OUR LIVES ON THE CAFETERIA PLAN —
SELF-SERVICE ONLY.

* * *

THE COACH

A coach there was and he made his prayer
 (Even as you and I)
To a bat and a ball and years of strife
Only to feel the Critics' knife
But the fool called it his way of life.
 (Even as you and I)

Oh the years we waste and the tears we waste
And the work of head and hand
belong to the poor coach who did not know
 (And now he knows he will never know)
And cannot understand

A coach there was and the time he spent
 (Even as you and I)
To teach a quarterback with good intent
But the boy called a play that was not meant
 (Even as you and I)

Oh the play we lost and the game we lost
Though excellent things were planned
Belongs to the Coach who didn't know why
And now we know he will never know why
And cannot understand

The Coach was stripped of all his pride
 (Even as you and I)
When the fans of the team threw him aside
Though some of him lived, most of him died
 (Even as you and I)

Oh, why can't the game ever be won
With a last minute hit or goal
And isn't the blame and isn't the shame
That strings the Coach like a red-hot coal
It's coming to know he will never know
And will never understand . . . .

* * *

**IF YOU ARE MADE OF THE RIGHT STUFF, A HARD FALL RESULTS
IN A HIGH BOUNCE.**

* * *

The minute you get the idea you're indispensable, you aren't.

* * *

THERE IS NO MISTAKE SO GREAT AS THE MISTAKE OF NOT GOING ON . . .

VII. LOSING * QUITTING

MR. MEANT TO — HAS A COMRADE AND HIS NAME IS DIDN'T — DO. HAVE YOU EVER MET THEM? DID THEY EVER CALL ON YOU? THESE TWO FELLOWS LIVE TOGETHER IN THE HOUSE OF NEVER WIN AND I AM TOLD THAT IT IS HAUNTED BY THE GHOST OF COULD — HAVE — BEEN.

* * *

PROLONGED IDLENESS PARALYZES INITIATIVE.

* * *

THE STUFF

The test of a man is the fight he makes,
the grit that he daily shows,
The way he stands on his feet and takes
Fate's numerous bumps and blows.
A coward can smile when there's naught to fear,
When nothing his progress bars,
But it takes a man to stand and cheer
While some other fellow soars.

It isn't the victory after all,
But the fight that a brother makes;
The man, who, driven against a wall,
Still stands up erect and takes
The blows of fate with his head up high,
Bleeding and bruised and pale,
Is the man who will win in the by and by,
For he ain't afraid to fail.

It's the bumps you get and the jolts you get,
And the shocks that your courage stands,
The hours of sorrow and vain regret,
The prize that escaped your hands,
That test your mettle and prove your worth,
It isn't the blows you deal,
But the blows you take on the good old earth
That show if your stuff is real.

* * *

It is defeat that turns bone to flint, it is defeat that turns muscle to gristle, it is defeat that makes men invincible.

* * *

EXPERIENCE IS A WONDERFUL THING. IT ENABLES YOU TO RECOGNIZE A MISTAKE WHEN YOU MAKE IT AGAIN.

* * *

A PARROT TALKS MUCH BUT FLIES LITTLE.

VII. LOSING * QUITTING

A second rate man can never make a first class ball player.

J.S. White

* * *

FROM THE CAMP OF THE BEATEN

by Grantland Rice

I have learned something well worth while
That victory could not bring —
To wipe the blood from my mouth and smile
Where none can see the sting'
I can walk, head up, while my heart is down
From the beating that brought its good,
And that means more than the champion's crown
Who is taking the easier road.

I have learned something worth far more
Than victory brings to men;
battered and beaten, bruised and sore,
I can still come back again;
Crowded back in the hard, tough race,
I've found that I have the heart
To look raw failure in the face
And train for another start.

Winners who wear the victor's wreath,
Looking for softer ways,
Watch for my blade as it leaves the sheath.
Sharpened on rougher days,
Trained upon pain and punishment,
I've groped my way through the night,
But the flag still flies from my battle tent
And I've only begun to fight . . .

* * *

WHEN THINGS GO WRONG

I count it best, when things go wrong,
to hum a tune and sing a song;
a heavy heart means sure defeat,
but joy is victory replete.

If skies are cloudy, count the gain,
new life depends upon the rain;
the cuckoo carols loud and long
when clouds hang low and things go wrong.

When things go wrong, remember then
the happy heart has strength of ten;
forget the sorrow, sing a song —
it makes all right when things go wrong.

Charles Henry Chelsey

VII. LOSING * QUITTING

Some men are built upside down — their feet smell and their nose runs.

* * *

STICK IT OUT

When your world's about to fall,
And your back's against the wall,
When you're facing wild retreat and utter rout;
When it seems that naught can stop it,
All your pleas and plans can't prop it
Get a grip upon yourself and — stick it out!

Any craven fool can quit,
But a man with pluck and grit,
Will hold until the very final shout;
In the snarling teeth of sorrow
He will laugh and say "Tomorrow
The luck will change — I guess I'll stick it out."

The luck does change; you know it;
All the records prove and show it,
And the men who win are men who strangle doubt,
Who hesitate nor swerve,
Who have grit and guts and nerve,
And whose motto is: Play hard, and stick it out.

And you think you can't last long,
So you, when things go wrong,
That you've got to quit nor wait for the final bout;
Smile, smile at your beholders,
Clench your teeth and square your shoulders and fight!
You'll win if you but STICK IT OUT!!

* * *

HE WHO LOSES **MONEY** LOSES MUCH;
HE WHO LOSES **FRIENDS,** LOSES MORE;
HE WHO LOSES **FAITH,** LOSES ALL.

* * *

IF YOU THINK YOU'RE **CONFUSED,** CONSIDER POOR COLUMBUS.
HE DIDN'T KNOW WHERE HE WAS GOING. **WHEN** HE GOT THERE,
HE DIDN'T KNOW WHERE HE WAS. **AND** WHEN HE GOT BACK **HE**
DIDN'T KNOW WHERE HE HAD BEEN.

* * *

The reason some men do not succeed is because their
wishbone is where their *backbone* ought to be.

* * *

THE STANDS ARE FOR SPECTATORS, NOT THE PLAYING FIELD.
FRANK BROYLES

VII. LOSING * QUITTING

When you think you're at the end of your rope —
tie a knot in it and hang on.

* * *

YOU CAN'T KEEP TROUBLE FROM COMING, BUT YOU NEEDN'T GIVE IT A CHAIR TO SIT ON.

* * *

If you indulge in self pity, the only sympathy you
can expect is from the same source.

* * *

LIFE is not easy for any of us, but it is a continued challenge, and it is up
to us to be cheerful and to be strong, so that those who depend on us may
draw strength from our example.

* * *

THE INDISPENSABLE MAN

*Sometime when you're feeling important, sometime when your ego's
in bloom, sometime when you take it for granted you're the best
qualified in the room. Sometime when you feel your going would
leave an unfillable hole, just follow this simple instruction and see
how it humbles your soul.*

*Take a bucket and fill it with water, put your hand in up to your
wrist, take it out — and the hole that's remaining is a measure of how
you'll be missed. You can splash all you please as you enter, you can
stir up the water galore, but stop, and you'll see in a minute that it
looks quite the same as before.*

*There's a moral in this quaint expression, just do the best that you
can, be proud of yourself, but remember ther is no indispensable
man.*

* * *

A PERSON IS ABOUT AS BIG AS THE THINGS THAT MAKE HIM ANGRY.

* * *

Following the path of least resistance
is what makes men and rivers crooked.

* * *

DON'T LEAVE ANY REGRETS ON THE FIELD.

VII. LOSING * QUITTING

IF LESSONS ARE LEARNED IN DEFEAT AS THEY SAY, OUR TEAM IS REALLY
GETTING A GREAT EDUCATION.

MURRAY WARMATH

* * *

Crying over spilt milk does nothing but make a bigger
mess to clean up.

* * *

ANYTIME YOU FEEL LIKE QUITTING

*Throughout your career, perhaps you'll remember this story of one of
our people:*
   He failed in business in '32.
   He ran as a state legislator and lost in '32.
   He tried business again and failed in '33.
   His sweetheart died in '35.
   He had a nervous breakdown in '36.
   He ran for state elector in '40 after he regained his health.
   *He was defeated for congress in '43, defeated again for
   congress in '48, defeated when he ran for senate in '55 and
   defeated for vice president of the United States in '56.*
   He ran for the senate again in '58 and lost.
   This man never quit.
   He kept trying til the last.
   *In 1860, this man, Abraham Lincoln, was elected President of the
United States of America.*

* * *

The Call Of The Wild

You're sick of the game, why, that's a shame; you're young, you're brave
and you're bright. You have had a raw deal, I know, but don't squeal,
buck up! Do your darndest and fight! It's the plugging away that will win
you the day. So don't be a piker 'ole pard; just call on your grit, it's so
easy to quit. It's keeping on living that's hard.

It's easy to cry that you're beaten, and die. It's easy to crawfish and
crawl, but to fight and to fight when hopes out of sight, why, that's the best
game of them all. And although you come out of each grueling bout all
broken and beaten and scarred, just give one more try; it's so easy to die,
it's keeping your chin up that's hard.

Robert Service

* * *

THE BEST ERASER IN THE WORLD IS A GOOD NIGHT'S SLEEP.

VII. LOSING * QUITTING

WE ALL MAKE MISTAKES — ESPECIALLY THOSE WHO DO THINGS.

* * *

PLAYING THE GAME

So you played the game, and you lost, my lad?
And you're battered and bleeding too.

And your hopes are dead and your heart is lead.
And your whole world's sad and blue.

And you sob and cry in your grief and your pain
for the hopes that had to die. But the game is through
and it's up to you to laugh, though you want to cry.

For someone there must lose, my lad it's sad but
it's always true. And day by day in the games you play
it's sure sometimes to be you. So grit your teeth to
the pain, my lad for you battled the best you could.
And there's never shame, in the losing game when you lose
like a real man should.

For after all, life is a game, my lad, and we play
it as best we may. We win or lose as the gods may choose,
who govern the games we play.

But whether we win or lose, my lad, at the end when
the battle's through, we must wait with a smile for the
after while and the chances that will come anew. . .

* * *

MEN DO NOT FAIL, THEY JUST GIVE UP EASY.

* * *

FOUR THINGS NEVER COME BACK —
THE SPOKEN WORD
THE SPED ARROW
THE PAST LIFE
AND THE NEGLECTED OPPORTUNITY.

* * *

It's a lot tougher to be a football coach than a president. You've got four years as a president, and they guard you. A coach doesn't have anyone to protect him when things go wrong.

Harry Truman

* * *

Quitting is easy, fighting is hard
Quitting is losing, fighting is winning.

Buck Nystrom

VII. LOSING * QUITTING

CONCEIT IS A QUEER DISEASE. IT MAKES EVERYONE SICK
EXCEPT THE ONE WHO HAS IT.

* * *

When looking back, usually I'm more sorry for the things I didn't do than for the things I shouldn't have done.

* * *

WHY WORRY?

There are only two things to worry about; either you are well or you are sick. If you are well, then there is nothing to worry about. But if you are sick, there are two things to worry about; either you will get well, or you will die. If you get well, there is nothing to worry about. If you die, there are only two things to worry about; either you will go to Heaven or Hell. If you go to Heaven, there is nothing to worry about. But if you go to Hell, you'll be so busy shaking hands with friends you won't have to worry.

* * *

There's no thrill in easy sailing, when the skies are clear and blue. There's no joy in merely doing things which anyone can do. But there is some satisfaction that is mighty sweet to take, when you reach a destination that you thought you couldn't make!

* * *

ALL FOR THE BEST

Sometimes the sky is overcast . . . And I am feeling blue . . . And as the hours wander by . . . I know not what to do . . . And sometimes there is tragedy . . . To meet me at the door . . . And I must wonder whether life . . . Is worth my fighting for . . . But always there is some way out . . . And I have come to know . . . That brighter things will comfort me . . . In just a day or so . . . And I have learned that what is past . . . Was purposeful and good . . . But in my bed of bitterness . . . It was misunderstood . . . There is a certain destiny . . . In every human quest . . . Because when anything goes wrong . . . It happens for the best.

* * *

UNLESS YOU TRY TO DO SOMETHING BEYOND WHAT YOU HAVE
ALREADY DONE AND MASTERED, YOU WILL NEVER GROW . . .

* * *

When success turns a person's head, he's facing failure.

VII. LOSING * QUITTING

A JOB DONE POORLY STANDS AS A WITNESS AGAINST THE MAN WHO DID IT.

* * *

What Are You Doing Now?

It matters not if you lost the fight
  and were badly beaten too.
It matters not if you failed outright
  in the things you tried to do.
It matters not if you toppled down
  from the azure heights of blue,
But what are you doing now????

It matters not if your plans were foiled
  and your hopes have fallen through.
It matters not if your chance was spoiled
  for the gain almost in view.
It matters not if you missed the goal
  though you struggled brave and true . . .
But what are you doing now????

It matters not if your fortune's gone
  and your fame has vanished too.
It matters not if a cruel world's score
  be directed straight at you.
It matters not if the worst has come
  and your dreams have not come true . . .
But what are you doing now????

R. Rhodes Stabley

* * *

Success is never permanent. And fortunately, neither is failure . . .

* * *

WE ARE ALL MANUFACTURERS — SOME MAKE GOOD
OTHERS MAKE TROUBLE
AND STILL OTHERS MAKE EXCUSES.

* * *

Setbacks never whip a fighter.

* * *

ANY FOOL CAN CRITICIZE, CONDEMN, COMPLAIN — AND MOST FOOLS DO!

DALE CARNEGIE

* * *

Nothing is opened by mistake as often as one's mouth.

VII. LOSING * QUITTING

It is not because things are difficult that we do not dare;
it is because we do not dare that they are difficult.

Seneca

* * *

MACHO DOES NOT PROVE MUCHO —

* * *

Peace comes not from the absence of conflict in life
but from the ability to cope with it.

* * *

IF EVERYTHING IS GOING YOUR WAY,
YOU ARE PROBABLY HEADING IN THE WRONG DIRECTION.

* * *

**I cannot give you a formula for success, but I can give you the formula
for failure — which is: _Try to please everybody._**

Herbert Bayard Swope

* * *

SOME PEOPLE WHO SLAP YOU ON THE BACK ARE TRYING TO HELP
YOU SWALLOW WHAT THEY JUST TOLD YOU.

* * *

Failure is something you know in your heart. Success is something that lies
in the eye of the beholder.

* * *

EXCUSES ARE LIKE BELLY BUTTONS: EVERYBODY HAS ONE.

* * *

_Every great improvement has come after repeated failures.
Virtually nothing comes out right the first time.
Failures, repeated failures, are fingerposts on the road
to achievement._

Charles F. Kettering

* * *

THE TROUBLE WITH THIS WORLD IS THAT TOO MANY PEOPLE TRY
TO GO THROUGH LIFE WITH A CATCHER'S MIT ON BOTH HANDS.

* * *

Defeat must be _faced_, but it need not be _final_.

VII. LOSING * QUITTING

THERE IS NO SADDER SIGHT THAN A YOUNG PESSIMIST.

MARK TWAIN

* * *

To him who tries and fails and quits—
I am the foul blow.
But, to him who in defeat,
the lessons of life would learn—
I lead through darkness and disaster
To where the scarlet lights of triumph burn.

* * *

The brave man is not he who feels no fear, for that were stupid and irrational; but he whose noble soul its fears subdues and bravely dares the danger nature shrinks from.

Basil

* * *

AFTER ALL IS SAID AND DONE, THERE'S A LOT MORE SAID THAN DONE.

* * *

If things are not going well with you, begin correcting the situation by carefully examining the service you are rendering, and especially the spirit in which you are rendering it.

Roger Babson

* * *

GIVING UP IS THE ULTIMATE TRAGEDY.
Robert J. Donovan

* * *

Don't waste time in doubts and fears; spend yourself in the work before you, well assured that the right performance of this hour's duties will be the best preparation for the hours or ages that follow it.

Emerson

* * *

THE ONLY THINGS THAT EVOLVE BY THEMSELVES IN AN ORGANIZATION ARE **DISORDER, FRICTION** AND **MALPERFORMANCE.**

* * *

MOST ANYTHING IN LIFE IS EASIER TO GET INTO THAN OUT OF.

VII. LOSING * QUITTING

A MAN BEGINS CUTTING HIS WISDOM TEETH THE FIRST TIME
HE BITES OFF MORE THAN HE CAN CHEW.

* * *

CAN'T

CAN'T is the worst word that's written or spoken;
Doing more harm here than slander and lies;
On it is many a strong spirit broken,
And with it many a good purpose dies.
It springs from the lips of the thoughtless each morning
And robs us of courage we need through the day.
It rings in our ears like a timely-sent warning
And laughs when we falter and fall by the way.

CAN'T is the father of feeble endeavor,
The parent of terror and half-hearted work;
It weakens the efforts of artisans clever,
And makes of the toiler an indolent shirk.
It poisons the soul of the man with a vision;
It stifles in infancy many a plan;
It greets honest toiling with open derision
And mocks at the hopes and the dreams of a man.

CAN'T is a word none should speak without blushing;
To utter it should be a symbol of shame;
Ambition and courage it daily is crushing;
It blights a man's purpose and shortens his aim,
Despise it with all of your hatred of error;
Refuse it the lodgement it seeks in your brain;
Arm against it as a creature of terror,
And all that you dream of you some day shall gain.

CAN'T is the word that is foe to ambition,
An enemy ambushed to shatter your will;
Its prey is forever the man with a mission
And bows but to courage and patience and skill.
Hate it, with hatred that's deep and undying,
For once it is welcomed 'twill break any man;
Whatever the goal you are seeking, keep trying
And answer this demon by saying, "I CAN."

Edgar A. Guest

* * *

If you never take a chance, you will never be defeated —
But you will never accomplish anything either.

* * *

EVERYONE WILL GET BEAT SOMETIME PHYSICALLY BUT A **CHAMPION** SELDOM GETS BEAT **MENTALLY**.

CHUCK KNOLL

VII. LOSING * QUITTING

WHEN A MAN IMAGINES THAT HE HAS ATTAINED PERFECTION
HIS DECLINE BEGINS.

* * *

**A man cannot be polished without friction . . .
Nor a man perfected without trials.**

* * *

—It's All In A State of Mind—

If you think you are beaten, you are; if you think you dare not, you won't; If you like to win, but don't think you can, it's almost a cinch you won't.

If you think you'll lose, you're lost; for out in the world you'll find success begins with a fellow's will. It's all in a state of mind.

For many a game is lost ere even a play is run, and many a coward fails ere even his work is begun.

Think big and your deeds will grow, think small and you'll fall behind; think that you can and you will; It's all in a state of mind.

If you think you are out-classed you are; you've got to think high to rise; you've got to be sure of yourself before you can ever win a prize.

Life's battles don't always go to the stronger or faster man, but sooner or later, the man who wins is the fellow who thinks he can.

Walter D. Wintle

* * *

IF YOU NEVER HAVE FAILED, IT'S AN EVEN GUESS YOU NEVER
HAVE WON A HIGH SUCCESS.

* * *

There is so much that is bad in the best of us, and so much that is good in the worst of us, that it doesn't behoove any of us, to talk about the rest of us.

* * *

ARE YOU PART OF THE **PROBLEM** OR PART OF THE **SOLUTION?**

* * *

THE LOAD OF TOMORROW, ADDED TO THAT OF YESTERDAY,
CARRIED
TODAY, MAKES THE STRONGEST FALTER.

SIR WILLIAM OSLER

VII. LOSING * QUITTING

A MAN WHO MAKES A MISTAKE AND DOES NOT CORRECT IT IS COMMITTING ANOTHER.

CONFUCIUS

* * *

PRESS ON

Nothing in the world can take the place of persistence.

Talent will not; nothing is more common than unsuccessful men with talent.
Genius will not; unrewarded genius is almost a proverb.
Education will not; the world is full of educated derelicts.

Persistence and determination alone are omnipotent.

* * *

"Luck is always against the man who depends on it."

* * *

WHEN THE PRESSURE'S ON

How do you act when the pressure's on,
When the chance for victory's almost gone,
When Fortune's star has refused to shine,
When the ball is on your five-yard line?

How do you act when the going's rough,
Does your spirit lag when breaks are tough?
Or, is there in you a flame that glows
Brighter as fiercer the battle grows?

How hard, how long will you fight the foe?
That's what the world would iike to know!
Cowards can fight when they're out ahead!
The up hill grind shows a thoroughbred!

You wish for success? — Then tell me, son,
How do you act when the pressure's on?

VII. LOSING * QUITTING

To Any Athlete

Why is it each is the last to find
That his legs are gone — that his eyes are bad,
That the quicker reflexes have left his mind,
That he hasn't the stuff that he one day had,
That lost youth mocks, and he doesn't see
The ghost of the fellow that used to be?

How can they slip from the heights so far
And never know that the day has gone
When their eyes were fixed on a rising star
With a firm foundation to stand upon?
How can they slip as the comets fall
And read no writing upon the wall?

Caught by a stride which they used to beat —
Nailed by a punch that they used to block —
Trailing the flurry of flying feet,
But dreaming still of the peaks that mock —
Each is the last to learn from fate
That his story is finished and out of date.

* * *

THE LAGGARD'S EXCUSE

He worked by day
And toiled by night,
He gave up play
And some delight.

Dry books he'd read
New things to learn
And forged ahead,
Success to earn.

He plodded on
With faith and PLUCK,
And when he won
Men called it LUCK . . .

* * *

Failure is the line of least persistence.

* * *

Some people are so busy learning the tricks of the trade
that they never learn the trade.

* * *

Anger is only one letter short of danger.

* * *

No trial would trouble you if you knew God's purpose in sending it.

Winning Words

Chapter VIII

Teamwork
Unity

VIII. TEAMWORK * UNITY

NO TEAM HAS A CORNER ON HARD WORK, DESIRE AND ENTHUSIASM.

DUFFY DAUGHERTY

* * *

I carry a link in my pocket
A simple reminder to me
Of the fact that I am a team member
No matter where I may be.

This little link is not magic
Nor is it a good luck charm
It isn't meant to protect me
From every physical harm.
It's simply an understanding
Between my teammates and me.

When I put my hand in my pocket
To bring out a coin or key
The link is there to remind me
Of what a team member should be.

It links me to the team
It links me to the school
It is a constant reminder
That there is no place for a fool.

So I carry this link in my pocket
To remind me many a time
That a man without conviction
Isn't worth a simple dime.

Norm Parker

* * *

Remember This

If you **work** for a man, in Heaven's name, **work** for him. If he pays you wages which supply you bread and butter, **work** for him; speak well of him; stand by him and the institutions he represents. If you must vilify, condemn and eternally disparage — resign your position, and when you are outside, damn to your heart's content, but as long as you are part of the institution do not condemn it. If you do, you are loosening the tendrils that are holding you to the institution, and at the first high wind, you will be unprotected and blown away, and will probably never know why.

Elbert Huggard

* * *

IF YOU MUST KICK — KICK TOWARDS THE GOAL.

BOB DEVINE

VIII. TEAMWORK * UNITY

IT IS SO EASY FOR US TO JUSTIFY OUR OWN
INEFFICIENCIES BY CRITICIZING OTHERS . . .

* * *

These things are necessary on your squad to allow the players to feel committed to the game:

1. *A sincere, wholesome respect for one another.*
2. *A feeling of sensitivity by the coaches to the academic, social, etc., problems of the student athlete.*
3. *A sincere desire to help the student athlete.*
4. *Fairness-honesty — the players cannot feel — the reason I'm not playing is coach doesn't like me.*
5. *Maybe the most important — there are enough people sitting around the locker room to say to the guy who is always complaining — Quit your bitching and get to work!*

Dan Devine

* * *

It isn't the plays or the system that gets the job done, it's the quality of the people in the system.

Joe Paterno

* * *

Teamwork is giving with no thought of receiving.
It's being sincere and in sincerity believing.
It's someone to talk to and someone talking to you.
It's telling and hearing what is true.
It's refusing to believe that bad exists.
It's knowing that when not around you are missed.
It's trying to help any way you can if even it's only to understand.
It's a willingness to learn how to give more.
It's getting it done without keeping score.
It's trusting in faith each and every day.
It's knowing you rate in a very special way.

* * *

**THERE ARE FEW, IF ANY, JOBS IN WHICH *ABILITY ALONE* IS SUFFICIENT.
NEEDED ALSO ARE *LOYALTY, SINCERITY, ENTHUSIASM* AND *COOPERATION.***

* * *

It takes less time to do a thing *right*
than it does to explain why you did it *wrong*.

VIII. TEAMWORK * UNITY

THE BEST THING TO HOLD ONTO IN LIFE IS EACH OTHER.

* * *

TEAMWORK

The world is full of problems,
There's much to cause distress;
We all are bowed beneath the cares
That daily round us press.
There's only one solution,
'Tis simply stated thus:
"A little less of you or me,
A little more of us."

The rule of each one for himself
Most foolish is to follow;
It brings no savor to the game,
Its victories are hollow.
But the other plan has never failed
To bring satisfaction, plus:
"A litle less of you or me,
A little more of us."

A flake of snow is very small,
'Tis lost to sight quite quickly;
But many flakes combined will fill
The roads and pathways thickly.
United we can face the fight
Without distress or fuss:
"A little less of you or me,
A little more of us."

William T. Card

* * *

A HEAD COACH IS GUIDED BY THIS MAIN OBJECTIVE: DIG, CLAW, WHEEDLE, COAX THAT FANATICAL EFFORT OUT OF THE PLAYERS. YOU WANT YOUR TEAM TO PLAY ON SATURDAY AS IF THEY WERE PLANTING THE FLAG ON IWO JIMA.

DARRELL ROYAL

* * *

The team that makes the fewest mistakes usually wins the game.

* * *

The team that **won't** be **beaten can't** be **beaten.**

Frank Broyles

* * *

Please all and you please none.

VIII. TEAMWORK * UNITY

THE MAN WHO ROWS THE BOAT GENERALLY DOESN'T HAVE TIME TO ROCK IT.

* * *

—Team Work—

*It's all very well to have courage and skill and its
fine to be counted a star, but the single deed with
it's touch of thrill doesn't tell us the man you are;
for there's no lone hand in the game we play, we must
work to a bigger scheme, and the thing that counts in
the world today is how do you pull with the team?*

*They may sound your praise and may call you great,
they may single you out for fame, but you must work
with your running mate or never you'll win the game.
For never the work of life is done by the man with a
selfish dream, for the battle is lost or the battle is won
by the spirit of the team.*

*You may think it's fine to be praised for skill. But
a greater thing to do is to set your mind and your
will on the goal that's just in view; it's helping
your fellow man to score when his chances hopeless
seem, it's forgetting self till the game is o'er and
fighting for the team.*

* * *

NO MAN IS AS IMPORTANT AS THE TEAM.

* * *

FOOTBALL TEAMS HAVE THREE TYPES OF PLAYERS
1. Those **willing** and **able**
2. Those **able** and **not willing**
3. Those **willing** and **not able.**

* * *

In order to have a winner, the team must have a feeling of unity; every
player must put the team first ahead of personal glory.

Bear Bryant

* * *

There is no **"I"** in the word team.

* * *

EVERY MAN ON THE TEAM HAS A RIGHT TO PLAY . . .
SOME MORE THAN OTHERS.

WHAT IS FOOTBALL?   BY TONTO COLEMAN

It's a wild and wonderful combination of intelligence, dumbness, speed, agility and a large helping of violence.

Outsiders may be thrilled by the spectacle of football but non-combatants will never fully know what the game really means to those who risk their bones to play it. Only a participant can understand its true nature. Only a man who has left a little of himself on the field can love football with a religious passion.

Football is not a game where losing is tolerated, for even a second. It is a game of oaths and slogans and battle cries. The emphasis is always on winning, regardless of the naive poems about "playing the game." The coach who strings victories together as a diamond necklace is coddled like an Oriental despot. It is the way the code operates. Everyone understands that stragglers are shot.

What is football?

It is a shocking upset every now and then. It is Chicken Little Tech rising in a mighty wrath and blowing Moose Jaw U out of the Top Ten. It is some skinny sophomore who wants to play making a second stringer of last year's All-American who thought he had it made.

What is football?

It is a 10-year professional, just retired, showing a sportswriter the place where his right knee bones used to be. It is foul weather on the last weekend and season-ticket-holders huddled together, insanely risking their health to see that sophomore halfback break the school rushing record. And football is a big lug of a left tackle croaking in the Alma Mater on graduation day with tears leaking down his beefy, battered cheeks, already worrying about how he'll feel next season when he has to wear wing-tips instead of cleats.

* * *

EQUAL OPPORTUNITY FOR *ALL* SPECIAL PRIVILEGES FOR *NONE.*

* * *

The amount that be can consumed and executed by a team is controlled by the weakest man on it . . . And while others can give him physical help, he has to do his own thinking.

* * *

WHAT REALLY COUNTS IS NOT THE NUMBER OF HOURS YOU PUT IN, BUT HOW MUCH YOU PUT IN THE HOURS.

VIII. TEAMWORK * UNITY

PEOPLE WITH LITTLE INTELLIGENCE GENERALLY ARE **SELFISH** AND VICE VERSA.

* * *

—INTENSITY—

"I"   Energy — correctly applied in team effort.
"N"   Noise — not by mouth, but by action.
"T"   Training — keep the team rules.
"E"   Energy — correctly applied in team effort.
"N"   Need — the great need for pride.
"S"   Sacrifice — the team comes first.
"I"   Intelligence — be smart not smart aleck.
"T"   Thoroughness — details are important.
"Y"   You — are very important.

* * *

The best way to forget your own problems
is to help someone else solve theirs.

* * *

Roger Bacon H.S., Cincinnati, Ohio —Bron Bacevich—

We emphasize the following to each of our players:

1. The importance of being on time.
2. Control of temper.
3. Meaning of loyalty and self-sacrifice.
4. Exercising good judgement.
5. Strict discipline.
6. Individual responsibility.
7. Sportsmanship and fair play.
8. Pride in oneself and in others.
9. Burning desire to excell.
10. Respect of authority.

* * *

BUILD FOR YOUR TEAM A *FEELING OF ONENESS*, OF DEPENDANCE
UPON ONE ANOTHER AND OF STRENGTH TO BE DERIVED BY UNITY.

VINCE LOMBARDI

* * *

One of the rarest things that a man ever does is the very best he can . . .

* * *

Teamwork teaches that each member of the organization must sacrifice
for another — for the good of everyone.

Frank Leahy

VIII. TEAMWORK * UNITY

THE REAL WAY TO ENJOY LIFE, IS AS A PARTICIPANT. PERHAPS IT'S THE PEOPLE WHO THINK THEY'RE SPECTATORS SPREAD THE IDEA THAT ALL PLEASURE MUST BE PAID FOR. DON'T PAY FOR ANY OF IT . . . **LIFE IS FREE.**

* * *

When The Struggling Day Is Over

When the struggling day is over,
When 'twas win or lose it all,
When the victor's score is totaled,
And they wait the judge's call,
They will tell they did not conquer
Through pure luck or passing fame,
But because they lived their motto —
STICK TOGETHER; PLAY THE GAME.

It's a slogan for all victors
Why know the fight's not won
By those who pass up teamwork
And fire a lonely gun,
But each man is in position
At the summons of his name,
Goes crashing, slashing, fighting —
A PARTNER IN THE GAME.

Sometimes a lad must do it-
Play a lone single hand-
But when he works with others,
He has to understand
He's a partner to his teammates
And has lost all hope for fame
Unless he heeds the warning —
STICK TOGETHER; PLAY THE GAME!

* * *

CO-OPERATE—REMEMBER THE BANANA—EVERYTIME IT LEAVES THE BUNCH—IT GETS SKINNED!

* * *

We may have come in **different ships,** but we're all in the **same boat** now.

* * *

THE HIGHER YOU GO IN LIFE, THE MORE YOU BECOME DEPENDENT ON OTHERS.

* * *

A group becomes a team when each member is sure enough of himself and his contribution to praise the skills of the other.

Norman G. Shidle

VIII. TEAMWORK * UNITY

HOW TO BE A CHAMPION

1. Exude a surplus of confidence around your competitors and self at all times, but don't be unsportsmanlike.

2. Help your competitors at all times. After all, you might make a friend out of him.

3. STUDY-STUDY-STUDY

4. Question anyone you meet about his technique, how he trained, how to correct your troubles.

5. Compete as often as possible to get experience; don't compete for medals, but for fun and companionship.

6. Don't let yourself think about competing for second place, you came here to win.

7. Set a concrete goal for yourself, even if you think it's impossible. Nothing is impossible for a man with faith.

8. Be determined, irrespective of your size, shape, training state, equipment or conditions.

9. Always take the blame yourself for failure, study each failure with greater intensity than your success, you never learn anything when you win.

10. Control your emotions at all times in competition, it can completely destroy your timing and coordination.

11. Be critical, objective and open-minded at all times.

12. Don't drink or smoke at any time, the real champion would never do it and the others seldom do it.

13. Tell your coach what your problems seem to be and rely upon him to help you solve the difficulty.

14. Study the physiology of training, the psychology of your competitors and EXPERIMENT ALL THE TIME.

* * *

**The main ingredient of stardom —
is the rest of the team.**

Winning Words
Chapter IX

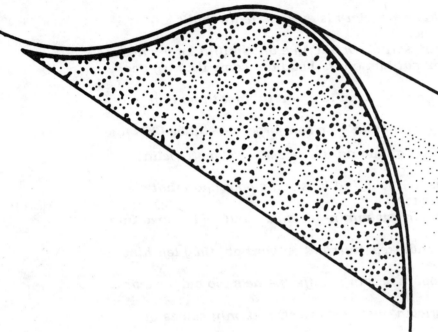

Winning
Success

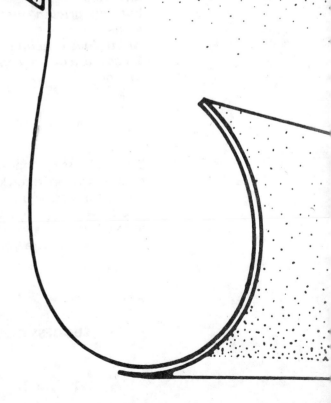

IX. WINNING * SUCCESS

THE LADDER OF SUCCESS DOESN'T CARE WHO CLIMBS IT.

FRANK TYGER

* * *

STUBBED HIS TOE

*Did ye ever pass a youngster 'et had gone an' stubbed
his toe,*
*An' was crying by th' roadside sort o' lonesome like
an' slow,*
*A 'holden' of his dusty foot, all hard an' brown an'
bare,*
*An' tryin' to keep fr'm his eyes th' tears that's
gatherin' there?*
Ye hear him sort o' sobbin' like an' snuffin' of his nose,
*Ye stop an' pat him on th' head an' some way try t'ease
his woes,*
*Ye treat him sort ' kind like, an' th' fust thing that
y' know,*
He's up an' off smilin' — clean forgot he stubbed his toe.

*Long th' road o' human life ye see a fellow travelin'
slow,*
*An' like as not ye'll find he's some poor chap that's
stubbed his toe*
*He was makin' swimmin' headway, but he bumped into
a stone,*
*An' his friends kep' hurryin' onward an' they left him
there alone.*
*He ain't sobbin' er ain't sniffin' — he's too old for tears
an' cries*
*but he's grievin' just as earnest, ef it only comes in
sighs,*
An' it does a heap o' god sometime, to go a little slow,
*To say a word o' comfort to th' man that's stubbed
his toe.*

Frank Tyger

* * *

Your success depends upon you. You have to steer your own
course. You have to do your own thing. You must make your
own decisions. You have to solve your own problems. Your
character is your handiwork. You have to write your own
record. You have to build your own monument — or dig your
own pit. Which are you doing?

B.C. Forbes

* * *

SUCCESS COMES IN CANS, NOT IN CAN'TS!

IX. WINNING * SUCCESS

TRUE SUCCESS IS OVERCOMING THE FEAR OF
BEING UNSUCCESSFUL.

* * *

"I don't say these things because I believe in the 'brute'
nature of man or that men must be brutalized to be com-
bative. I believe in God, and I believe in human decency. I
firmly believe that any man's finest hour — his greatest
fulfillment to all he holds dear — is that moment when he
has worked his heart out in a good cause and lies exhausted on the field of battle — victorious."

Vince Lombardi

* * *

REFEREES

Walter Fudjak, Jr.

I think that I shall never see
a satisfactory referee,
About whose head a halo shines,
whose merits rate reporters lines.
One who calls them as they are
and not as I should wish, by far.
A gent who'll sting the coach who yaps,
from Siwash Hi or Old Millsaps.
Poems are made by fools like me
but only God could referee.

* * *

The most important ingredient in your gym bag is your
attitude.

* * *

There is no thrill in easy sailing when the skies are clear and blue.
There is no joy in merely doing things which anyone can do.
But there is some satisfaction that is mighty sweet to take.
When you reach a destination that you thought you couldn't make.

* * *

THE PRICE OF VICTORY IS HIGH; **BLOOD, SWEAT, TEARS,
FRUSTRATION** AND SOMETIMES **DEFEAT.**

* * *

IF YOU DON'T HAVE SOME HUMOR WITH PRESSURE,
PRESSURE WILL WIN!

IX. WINNING * SUCCESS

Never — NEVER — Never — NEVER GIVE UP!

W. CHURCHILL

* * *

SECOND BEST

by Frances C. Thompson

There's plenty of praise for the fellow that wins,
And the one who's always the lead;
But little is said for the one left behind,
Who tried, but didn't succeed.

Not for him the acclaim, though the effort's the same,
And his courage was equally great.
He ran a good race, but somehow the pace
Made him only a minute too late.

He tries once again, his courage still high,
Running steadily, always the same.
This pace all through life, in peace or in strife,
Makes a winner in spite of the name.

* * *

I will persist until I succeed.

I was not delivered into this world in defeat,
nor does failure course in my veins.

I am not a sheep waiting to be prodded by my
shepherd.

I am a winner and I refuse to talk, to walk
with the sheep.

The slaughter house of failure is not my destiny.

I will persist until I succeed.

* * *

The **big game** of next week, month or year is being **Won**
or **Lost** right now!

* * *

Winning is important. *Winning* has a joy and discrete purity that cannot
be replaced by anything else.
Winning is important to everyone's sense of satisfaction and well-being.
It is not everything, but it is something powerful, indeed beautiful, in itself
— something as essential to the spirit as striving is to the character.

A. Bartlett Giamatti
President
Yale University

IX. WINNING * SUCCESS

TRUE SUCCESS IS THE ONLY THING THAT YOU CANNOT HAVE
UNLESS AND UNTIL YOU HAVE OFFERED IT TO OTHERS.

* * *

What is the Price of Success?

*To use all of your courage to force yourself
to concentrate on the problem at hand, to think of it
deeply and constantly, to study it from all angles and
to plan.*

*To have a high and sustained determination to
put over what you plan to accomplish, not if circumstances be favorable to its accomplishment, but in spite
of all adverse circumstances which may arise . . . and
nothing worthwhile has ever been accomplished without
some obstacles to overcome.*

*To refuse to believe that there are any
circumstances sufficiently strong to defeat you in the
accomplishment of your purpose.*

* * *

THE RULES FOR SUCCESS

1. Find your own particular talent.
2. Be big.
3. Be honest.
4. Live with enthusiasm.
5. Don't let your possessions possess you.
6. Don't worry about your problems.
7. Look up to people when you can—down to no one.
8. Don't cling to the past.
9. Assume your full share of responsibility in the world.
10. Strive to be happy.

* * *

Successful men make up their minds what they want and
then go after it with everything in them.

* * *

HE WHO HAS HEART HAS HOPE, AND HE WHO HAS HOPE HAS
EVERYTHING.

ARABIAN PROVERB

* * *

Success without honor is an unseasoned dish; it will satisfy your hunger,
but it won't taste good.

Joe Paterno

IX. WINNING * SUCCESS

THE WILL TO WIN IS WORTHLESS IF YOU DO NOT HAVE THE
WILL TO PREPARE.

* * *

We are what we repeatedly do . . . **Excellence,** then, is
not an act but a habit.

Aristotle

* * *

The dictionary is the only place **success** comes before **work.**

* * *

Success

Bessie A. Stanley

He has achieved success who has lived well, laughed often, and loved
much; who has gained the respect of intelligent men, and the love of little
children; who has filled his niche and accomplished his task; who has never
lacked appreciation of earth's beauty, or failed to express it; who has always
looked for the best in others and given the best he had; whose life was an
inspiration; whose memory a benediction.

* * *

SUCCESS IS GETTING WHAT YOU WANT, HAPPINESS IS WANTING WHAT YOU GET.

* * *

SUCCESS

Success is speaking words of praise
In cheering other people's ways,
In doing just the best you can
With every task and every plan.
It's silence when your speech would hurt.
Politeness when your neighbor's curt.
It's deafness when the scandal flows,
And sympathy with other's woes.
It's loyalty when duty calls,
It's courage when disaster falls,
It's patience when the hours are long;
It's found in laughter and in song;
It's in the silent time of prayer,
In happiness and in despair
In all of life and nothing less
We find the thing we call success.

IX. WINNING * SUCCESS

KEEP A-GOIN'

Do your darndest when you play,
Keep a-goin'.
To take it easy doesn't pay,
Keep a-goin'.
When the game is pretty tough,
Don't you ever holler "nuff,"
Show the world you have the stuff,
Keep a-goin'.
You only need a harder punch,
Keep a-goin'.
'Tain't no use to stand and whine
When they're coming through your line;
Hitch your trousers up and climb,
Keep a-goin'.
If the other team's on top,
Keep a-goin'.
That's just the time you must not stop,
Keep a-goin'.
'S'pose they stop 'most every play;
One good long run may win the day;
To get discouraged doesn't pay,
Keep a-goin'.
When it seems the game is lost,
Keep a-goin'.
Do not stop at any cost—
Keep a-goin'.
Don't ever think that you can't win it,
A fightin' team is always in it;
So don't let up a single minute,
Keep a-goin'.

* * *

Who Misses or Who Wins the Prize

William Makepeace Thackeray

Who misses or who wins the prize
Go lose or conquer, as you can;

But if you fall, or if you rise,
Be each, pray God, a gentleman.

* * *

A MAN'S HAPPINESS AND SUCCESS IN LIFE WILL DEPEND NOT SO MUCH
UPON WHAT HE HAS, OR UPON WHAT POSITION HE OCCUPIES AS UPON
WHAT HE IS, AND THE HEART HE CARRIES INTO HIS POSITION.

J.J. WILSON

* * *

Pride is the basis of winning football.

Darrell Royal

IX. WINNING * SUCCESS

IT'S GREAT TO BE GREAT, BUT IT'S GREATER TO BE HUMAN.

WILL RODGERS

* * *

THE OPTIMIST VS. THE PESSIMIST

by William Arthur Ward

The optimist turns the impossible into the possible;
the pessimist turns the possible into the impossible.
The optimist pleasantly ponders how high his kite will fly;
the pessimist woefully wonders how soon his kite will fall.
The optimist sees a green near every sand trap;
the pessimist sees a sand trap near every green.
The optimist looks at the horizon and sees an opportunity;
the pessimist peers into the distance and fears a problem.
To the optimist all doors have handles and hinges;
to the pessimist all doors have locks and latches.
The optimist promotes progress, prosperity and plenty;
the pessimist preaches limitations, liabilities and losses.
The optimist accentuates assets, abundance, and advantages;
the pessimist majors in mistakes, misfortunes and misery.
The optimist goes out and finds the bell;
the pessimist gives up and wrings his hands.

* * *

It ain't braggin' if you've done it.

* * *

IF YOU HAVE TRIED TO DO SOMETHING AND **FAILED,** YOU ARE VASTLY BETTER OFF
THAN IF YOU HAD TRIED TO DO NOTHING AND **SUCCEEDED.**

* * *

Once you've **won** or **lost,** it's behind you. What lies ahead is all that matters.

Bud Wilkinson

* * *

A SUCCESSFUL PERSON IS ONE WHO WENT AHEAD AND DID THE THING
THE REST OF US NEVER QUITE GOT AROUND TO.

* * *

The royal road to success would have more travelers if so many weren't
lost attempting to find short cuts.

H.C. Calvin

IX. WINNING * SUCCESS

Success if not a harbor but a voyage with its own perils to the spirit.

Richard Huger

* * *

WHEN YOUR ARMS ARE SO TIRED THAT YOU CAN HARDLY LIFT YOUR HANDS TO COME ON GUARD, *FIGHT ONE MORE ROUND.* WHEN YOUR NOSE IS BLEEDING AND YOUR EYES ARE BLACK AND YOU ARE SO TIRED THAT YOU WISH YOUR OPPONENT WOULD CRACK YOU ONE IN THE JAW AND PUT YOU TO SLEEP, *FIGHT ONE MORE ROUND* — REMEMBERING THAT THE MAN WHO ALWAYS FIGHTS *ONE MORE ROUND* IS NEVER WHIPPED.

JAMES J. CORBETT
Heavy Weight Champ

* * *

THE FINAL GOAL IS **WINNING . . .** ANYTHING THAT DISTRACTS FROM **WINNING** MUST BE DONE AWAY WITH.

GEORGE PERLES

* * *

A winning habit is like a cable . . . a thread is woven each day until the product becomes **UNBREAKABLE!!**

* * *

THE DIFFERENCE BETWEEN *CHAMP* AND *CHUMP* is "U".

* * *

57 Rules for Success
First, deliver the goods.
Second, the other **56** don't matter.

* * *

WORDS ARE LEAVES — DEEDS ARE FRUIT.

* * *

The path to success is never a 5 lane, no traffic, super highway. *Heartbreak, setbacks, frustrations, failures, enemies . . .*appear time and again to prevent you from reaching your goals.

N.C. Stone

* * *

IT IS IMPOSSIBLE TO GET A TOEHOLD ON SUCCESS BY ACTING LIKE A HEAL.

IX. WINNING * SUCCESS

ARE YOU STRONG ENOUGH TO HANDLE SUCCESS?

"Unfortunately, the road to anywhere is filled with many pitfalls, and it takes a man of determination and character not to fall into them. As I have said many times, whenever you get your head above the average, someone will be there to take a poke at you. That is to be expected in any phase of life. However, as I have also said many times before, if you see a man on top of a mountain, he didn't just light there! Chances are he had to climb through many difficulties and with a great expenditure of energy in order to get there, and the same is true of a man in any profession, be he a great attorney, a great minister, a great man of medicine or a great businessman. I am certain he worked with a definite plan and an aim and purpose in life. I have always thought that an excerpt from Parkenham Beatty's Self Reliance contained a good philosophy for each coach:

> *By your own soul learn to live,*
> *and if men thwart you, take no heed,*
> *if men hate you, have no care;*
> *Sing your song, dream your dream,*
> *hope your hope and pray your prayer.*

I am sure that if a coach will follow this philosophy of life, he will be successful. To sit by and worry about criticism, which too often comes from the misinformed or from those incapable of passing judgement on an individual or a problem, is a waste of time."

Adolph Rupp
Former University of Kentucky
Basketball Coach, Record High
874 Career Victories.

* * *

YOUR SHIP WON'T COME IN TILL YOU ROW OUT TO MEET IT.

* * *

In any test of skills we either get better or we slip backward. Start where you are with what you have; and make something better of it.

* * *

FOOTBALL MIRRORS LIFE

By Carl T. Rowan

. . . "America the nation can be not just a winner, but invincible, if its educators, business leaders, politicians and others will accept this lesson from the gridiron: *Talent, character, guts and other qualities of success do not come in a predetermined package — they simply are where you find them.*"

IX. WINNING * SUCCESS

WINNERS AND LOSERS; HOW THEY DIFFER

By Sydney Harris

Reprinted from the *Detroit Free Press*, January 9, 1967

1. A winner says, "Let's find out;" a loser says, "Nobody knows."

2. When a winner makes a mistake, he says, "It was my fault;" when a loser makes a mistake, he says, "It isn't my fault."

3. A winner credits his "good luck" for winning—even though it isn't good luck, a loser blames his "bad luck" for losing—even though it isn't bad luck

4. A winner knows how and when to say "Yes and No;" a loser says "Yes, but" and "Perhaps not" at the wrong times, and for the wrong reasons.

5. A winner isn't nearly as afraid of losing as a loser is secretly afraid of winning.

6. A winner goes through a problem; a loser goes around it, and never gets past it.

7. A winner makes a commitment; a loser makes promises.

8. A winner says, "I'm good, but not as good as I ought to be." A loser says, "I'm not as bad as a lot of other people."

9. A winner listens; a loser just waits until it's his turn to talk.

10. A winner feels strong enough to be gentle; a loser is never gentle—he is either weak or petty.

11. A winner respects those who are superior to him, and tries to learn something from them; a loser resents those who are superior to him, and tries to find chinks in their armor.

12. A winner explains; a loser complains.

13. A winner feels responsible for more than his job; a loser says, "I only work here."

14. A winner says, "There ought to be a better way to do it;" a loser says, "That's the way it's always been done."

15. A winner paces himself; a loser has only two speeds: hysterical and lethargic.

* * *

THE KISS SYSTEM OF TEACHING—

KEEP

 IT

  SIMPLE

   STUPID

IX. WINNING * SUCCESS

A MAN ATTAINS IN THE MEASURE THAT HE ASPIRES.

JAMES ALLEN

* * *

THE ONLY WAY TO WIN

It takes a little courage
And a little self-control,
And some grim determination,
If you want to reach your goal.
It takes a deal of striving,
And a firm and stern-set chin,
No matter what the battle,
If you really want to win.

There's no easy path to glory,
There's no rosy road to fame.
Life, however we may view it,
Is no simple parlor game;
But its prizes call for fighting,
For endurance and for grit;
For a rugged disposition
And a don't-know-when-to-quit.

You must take a blow or give one,
You must risk and you must lose,
And expect that in the struggle,
You will suffer from the bruise.
But you mustn't wince or falter,
If a fight you once begin;
Be a man and face the battle-
That's the only way to win.

* * *

Winners never quit, and quitters never win.

* * *

IT IS EASIER TO BECOME A CHAMPION THAN TO STAY A CHAMPION.

* * *

*Treat people nicely on the way up, you're liable
to meet them again on the way down.*

* * *

PRACTICE DOES NOT MAKE PERFECT!!
PERFECT PRACTICE MAKES PERFECT.

* * *

**THE WIND BLOWS THE STRONGEST UPON THOSE
WHO STAND THE TALLEST.**

F.C. HAYES

IX. WINNING * SUCCESS

SUCCESS CONSISTS OF DOING THE COMMON THINGS UNCOMMONLY WELL.

* * *

IF FOR BOYS

*If you can take the knowledge you have gathered
through years of study, work and school and turn it into
living acts of kindness through a life that keeps the
golden rule . . .*

*If you can give a little more than other fellows
and keep on trying though you're tired, yet make not
public all your efforts nor hold of account to be admired . . .*

*If you can keep on working toward the future
holding fast to all your secret goals though time and
circumstance may slow you and even strew your path with
burning coals . . .*

*If you to win a war, must lose a battle then lose it,
but let no one see you cry let sympathy be saved for
those who need it not for those who have the will to try . . .*

*If you can keep your trust in all things holy remembering,
too, that high above the power which made man still
directs him with infinite patience and with everlasting
love . . .*

*If you can dream and plan and struggle and keep
on when lesser men give in — you will have earned the
noble art of manhood and what's more, my son, you're
bound to win!*

* * *

Buck Nystrom's Four Corners of Success

1. COMMITMENT	2. EFFORT
SUCCESS	
3. MOTIVATION	4. DISCIPLINE

* * *

INSIDE INEFFICIENCY IS MORE TO BE FEARED THAN OUTSIDE COMPETITION.

* * *

EVERY SUCCESSFUL MAN I HAVE HEARD OF HAS DONE THE BEST HE COULD
WITH THE CONDITIONS AS HE FOUND THEM, AND NOT WAITED UNTIL NEXT YEAR
FOR BETTER.

E.W. HOWE

IX. WINNING * SUCCESS

CHANCE FAVORS THE PREPARED MIND.

LOUIS PASTEUR

* * *

IT TAKES ONLY TWO PERCENT

by Gene Emmet Clark, D.D.

Have you been working like a horse?
I've been thinking about that expression — and at least
one horse I can name has earned a pretty fair hourly
rate. Someone has figured out that the race horse,
Nashua, earned more than a million dollars in a total
racing time that added up to less than one-hour!

That's pretty good pay. Of course, we know that many
many more hours went into preparing for that winning hour
of racing.

But there is something else here that interests me.
What is there about a horse like Nashua that made him
such a consistent winner and made him so valuable?
You'd probably pay a hundred times as much for a horse
like Nashua as you would for an ordinary race horse.
but is he a hundred times faster? No. To be a consistent
winner and to be worth a hundred times as much as the average, he
needed only to be consistent in finishing just ahead of the rest.

All he had to do was win a good share of the time by a
nose to be worth a hundred times as much as an also-ran.
And so it is with human beings who are on top in the game of life.

A writer in a national magazine made the assertion that
the difference between the man of achievement and that man
of mediocrity is a difference of only about two percent in study, ap-
plication, interest, attention, and effort.
Only about two percent separates the winner from the loser!
A boxer can win the world's championship simply by winning one
more round than his oppponent—or even by being only a
point or two ahead. And this narrow margin can make the
difference between fame and fortune or never being heard
of again! It's often a matter of only two percent. We
have no idea of what a change we could make in our results
if we would simply add that two percent more time and
effort than the average person is willing to put in.

* * *

It is one thing to **itch** for something and another to **scratch** for it.

* * *

THE RACE IS NOT ALWAYS TO THE SWIFT BUT MOST OFTEN TO HIM WHO KEEPS ON RUNNING.

IX. WINNING * SUCCESS

**TIME CANNOT BE PURCHASED, MARKETED, OR SAVED.
IT CAN ONLY BE *SPENT*. THE SECRET, THEN, IS TO SPEND IT *WISELY*.**

* * *

WHAT IT TAKES TO BE NUMBER ONE

By Vince Lombardi

"Winning is not a sometime thing: it's an all-the-time thing. You don't win once in a while. You don't do things right once in a while. You do them right all the time. *Winning is a habit.* Unfortunately, so is losing.

There is no room for second place. There is only one place in my game and that is first place. I have finished second twice in my time at Green Bay and I don't ever want to finish second place again. There is a second place bowl game. But it is a game for losers played by losers. It is and always has been an American seal to be first in anything we do and to win and to win and to win.

Every time a football player goes out to ply his trade he's got to play from the ground up from the soles of his feet right up to his head. Every inch of him has to play. some guys play with their heads, that's O.K. You've got to be smart to be no. 1 in any business, but more important, you've got to play with your heart — with every fiber of your body. If you're lucky enough to find a guy with a lot of head and a lot of heart, he's never going to come off the field second.

Running a football team is no different from running any other kind of organization — an army, a political party, a business. The principles are the same. The object is to win — to beat the other guy. Maybe that sounds hard or cruel. I don't think it is.

It's a reality of life that men are competitive and the most competitive games draw the most competitive men. That's why they're there — to compete. they know the rules and the objectives when they get in the game. The objective is to win — fairly, squarely, decently, by the rules — but to win.

And in truth, I've never known a man worth his salt who in the long run, deep down in his heart, didn't appreciate the grind, the discipline. There is something in good men that really yearns for, needs, discipline and the harsh reality of head-to-head combat."

* * *

"IF AT FIRST YOU DON'T SUCCEED, YOU'RE DOING ABOUT AVERAGE.

Winning Words

Chapter X

Work

Education

X. WORK * EDUCATION

KEEP ON KEEPIN' ON

If the day looks kinder gloomy
    and your chances kinder slim,
    and the situation's puzzlin',
    and the prospect awful grim,
    and perplexities keep a-pressin'
    till all hope is nearly gone—
Just bristle up and grit your teeth
    and keep on keepin' on.

Fumin' never wins a fight,
    and frettin' never pays;
    There ain't no good in broodin' in
    those pessimistic ways;
    smile just kinder cheerfully
    when hope is nearly gone,
    and bristle up and grit your teeth
    and keep on keepin' on.

There ain't no use in growlin'
    and grumblin' all the time,
    when the music's ringin' everywhere,
    and everything's in rhyme;
    Just keep on smilin' cheerfully
    if hope is nearly gone,
    and bristle up and grit your teeth
    and keep on keepin' on.

* * *

The thing that makes a champion is obvious enough:
    It isn't any mystic prestidigitator's stuff.
It's nothing more than giving to whatever be the chore
    The power is in you — and a small scintilla more.

It isn't any wizardry, it's not a magic gift;
    It's merely lifting honestly the load you have to lift;
Or, in the game you're playing, it is using all your store of
    grit and nerve and energy — and just a trifle more.

The thing that makes a champion is simple, plain, and clear;
    it's never being "almost," "just about," or "pretty near."
It's summoning the utmost from your spirit's inner core and
    giving every bit of it — and just a little more.

"That little more — how much it is." As deep and wide and
    far as that enormous emptiness from molehill to a star,
The gulf between the earthbound and the eagles as they soar,
    THE CHAMPIONS GIVE THEIR BEST — AND ONE IOTA MORE.

* * *

**THE WORLD STANDS ASIDE TO LET ANYONE PASS
WHO KNOWS WHERE HE IS GOING.**

JORDAN

X. WORK * EDUCATION

NO ATHLETE WILL WORK FOR YOUR INTERESTS UNLESS THEY ARE HIS.

* * *

LET SOMETHING GOOD BE SAID

James W. Riley

When over the fair fame of friend or foe,
The shadow of disgrace shall fall; instead
Of words of blame, or proof of so and so,
Let something good be said.

Forget not that no fellow-being yet
May fall so low but love may lift his head;
Even the check of shame with tears is wet,
If something good be said.

No generous heart may vainly turn aside
In ways of sympathy; no soul so dead
But may awaken strong and glorified,
If something good be said.

And so I charge ye, by the thorny crown,
And by the cross on which the Savior bled,
And by your own soul's hope for fair renown,
Let something good be said.

* * *

Nine Ways To Change People Without Giving Offense or Arousing Resentment

1. Begin with praise and honest appreciation.

2. Call attention to people's mistakes indirectly.

3. Talk about your own mistakes before criticizing the other person.

4. Ask questions instead of giving orders.

5. Let the other man save his face.

6. Praise the slightest improvement and praise every improvement. Be hearty in your approbation and lavish in your praise.

7. Give the other person a fine reputation to live up to.

8. Use encouragement. Make the fault seem easy to correct.

9. Make the other person happy about doing the thing you suggest.

* * *

EVEN A MOSQUITO DOESN'T GET A SLAP ON THE BACK
UNTIL HE STARTS TO WORK.

X. WORK * EDUCATION

YOU CAN'T TURN BACK THE CLOCK.
BUT YOU CAN WIND IT UP AGAIN.

* * *

Are you playing the game on the field of life?
Are you keeping within the rules?
Do you play with a jump and a joy in the strife,
Nor whimper for better tools?

There is always a chap who lags behind,
And wails that the world is gray;
That his ax is dull, and his wheel won't grind,
And it's too late to begin today.

But if you should ask the other chap,
The one who has gone ahead,
You'll find that his tools were worse, mayhap;
And he's made new ones instead.

For playing the game means not to grin,
When the field is smooth and clear;
But to fight from the first for the joy therein,
Nor to heed the haunt of fear.

And though in the strife no prize you earn
That marks the victor's fame;
Know still, if you've tried at every turn,
You have won, for you've played the game!

Raymond Comstock

* * *

WHY ARE YOU TIRED? . . . . .

We have some absolutely irrefutable statistics that show why you are tired, and brother, it's no wonder you are tired. There aren't as many people working as you may have thought — at least according to this survey.

The population of this country is 200 million, but there are 62 million over 60 years of age. That leaves 138 million to do the work. People under 21 total 94 million — that leaves 44 million to do the work. Then there are 21 million who are employed by the government, which leaves 23 million to do the work, 10 million are in the armed forces which leaves 13 million to do the work. There are 12,800,000 in the state and city offices, leaving 200,000 to do the work. 126,000 in hospitals, etc., so that leaves 74,000 to do the work. However, 62,000 bums or vagrants refuse to work so that leaves 12,000. 11,998 are in jail, which leaves **2 people** to do the work — that's you and me brother, and I'm getting tired of doing **everything myself.**

* * *

A MAN WHO DARES TO WASTE ONE HOUR OF TIME
HAS NOT DISCOVERED THE VALUE OF LIFE.

CHARLES DARWIN

X. WORK * EDUCATION

Duties delayed are the devil's delight.

* * *

Make a good rule, and pray God to help you to keep it.
Never, if possible, lie down at night without being able to say:
I have made one human being, at least, a **little wiser,** a **little happier,**
or a **little better** this day.

Charles Kingsley

* * *

The *superior* man blames himself — the *inferior* man blames others.

Don Shula

* * *

INGENUITY, PLUS COURAGE, PLUS WORK EQUALS MIRACLES.

REV. BOB RICHARDS

* * *

When you affirm **big,** believe **big** and pray **big, big** things happen.

Norman Vincent Peale

* * *

WHICH ARE YOU?

A little more kindness
A little less speed,
A little more giving,
A little less greed,
A little more smile,
A little less frown,
A little less kicking,
A man while he's down,
A little more "We,"
A little less "I,"
A little more laugh,
A little less cry,
A little more flowers
On the pathway of life,
And fewer on graves
At the end of the strife.

* * *

THE TROUBLE WITH THE WORLD IS NOT THAT PEOPLE KNOW TOO LITTLE,
BUT THAT THEY KNOW SO MANY THINGS THAT AIN'T SO.

MARK TWAIN

X. WORK * EDUCATION

I often wonder what it is that brings one man success in life, and what it is that brings mediocrity or failure to his brother. The difference cannot be in mental capacity; there is not the difference in our mentalities indicated by the difference in performance. In short, I have reached the conclusion that some men succeed because they cheerfully pay the price of success, and others, though they claim ambition and a desire to succeed, are unwilling to pay that price.

* * *

What is the price of success? It is simply . . .

To use all of your courage to force yourself to concentrate on the problem at hand, to think of it deeply and constantly, to study it from all angles, and to plan.

To have a high and sustained determination to put over what you plan to accomplish, no matter what circumstances may arise . . . and nothing worthwhile has ever been accompalished without some obstacles overcome.

To refuse to believe that there are any circumstances sufficiently strong to defeat you in the accomplishment of your purpose.

HARD!! I should say so! That's why so many men never attempt to acquire success. They answer the siren call of the rut, and remain on the beaten paths for beaten men. Nothing worthwhile has ever been achieved without constant endeavor, some pain, and constant application of the lash of ambition. That's the price of success.

I believe every man should ask himself: Am I willing to endure the pain of this struggle for the comforts and the rewards and the glory that go with achievement? Or shall I accept the uneasy and inadequate contentment that comes with mediocrity? Am I willing to pay the price of success?

* * *

OPPORTUNITY

By Walter Malone

They do me wrong who say I come no more when once I knock and fail to find you in; For every day I stand outside your door, and bid you wake, and rise to fight and win.

Wail not for precious chances passed away, wail not for golden ages on the wane! Each night I burn the records of that day; and at sunrise every soul is born again.

* * *

YOUR INTEREST SHOULD BE IN THE FUTURE BECAUSE YOU'RE GOING TO SPEND THE REST OF YOUR LIFE THERE.

X. WORK * EDUCATION

IT TAKES MEN TO MAKE MEN

by S.I. Hayakawa

Never has it been so difficult for boys to grow up into men.

Becoming a man is not a matter of chronology. It is a matter of proof. Throughout the history of mankind, boys have had to prove themselves men.

To become a man it has always been necessary for boys to associate with men, as helpers on father's farm, as apprentices to craftsmen, as squires to knights, as water boys to baseball teams. Through such association they learn the secrets of the adult culture: what rituals to observe, how to care for equipment, how to drink and curse and fight, how to earn and maintain the respect of other men in a society of men.

But today most boys are separated from the lives of men. Men leave for factory or office early in the morning commuting many miles to work. They do not return until evening. Boys are brought up by mothers and school teachers.

Hence boys often have no ideas what their father do at work. They have no idea what a man does that makes him a man.

So the vast majority of boys are excluded from the world of men and denied the chance to exercise their powers. Physical or intellectual. Is it any wonder that there is a youth problem?

Boys need challenges. Their whole being cries out for them. To face starvation, the possibility of death at enemy hands, the risks of failure in school or work or business, and then to triumph over these dangers — these are the stuff of human growth, of maturity.

It takes men to make men. Mothers cannot do it by themselves. Nor can high schools. Nor colleges.

* * *

WHAT IS A FOOTBALL PLAYER?

By Charles Loftus

Between the innocence of boyhood and the dignity of manhood, we find a sturdy creature called a **football player.** Football players come in assorted weights, heights, jersey colors and numbers, but all football players have the same creed: to play every second of every game to the best of their ability.

continued

Football Player *continued*

Football players are found everywhere — underneath, on top of, running around, jumping over, passing by, twisting from or driving through the enemy. Teammates rib them, officials penalize them, students cheer them, kid brothers idolize them, coaches criticize them, high school girls adore them, alumni tolerate them, and mothers worry about them. A football player is courage in cleats, hope in a helmet, pride in pads, and the best of young manhood in moleskins.

When your team is behind, a football player is incompetent, careless, indecisive, lazy, uncoordinated and stupid. Just when your team threatens to turn the tide of battle, he misses a block, fumbles the ball, drops a pass, jumps offside, falls down, runs the wrong way, or completely forgets his assignment!

A football player is a composite — he eats like Notre Dame, but more often than not, plays like Grand Canyon High. To an opponent publicity man, he has the speed of a gazelle, the strength of an ox, the size of an elephant, the cunning of a fox, the agility of an adagio dancer, the quickness of a cat, and the ability of Red Grange, Glen Davis, Bronco Nagurski, and Jim Thorpe — Combined!

To his own coach he has, for press purposes, the stability of mush, the fleetness of a snail, the mentality of a mule, is held together by adhesive tape, baling wire, sponge rubber and has about as much chance of playing on Friday night as would his own grandmother.

To an alumnus a football player is someone who will never kick as well, run as far, block as viciously, tackle as hard, fight as fiercely, give as little ground, score as many points or generate nearly the same amount of spirit as did those particular players of his own yesteryear.

A football player likes game films, trips away from home, practice sessions without pads, hot showers, long runs, whirlpool baths, recovered fumbles, points after touchdowns, and the quiet satisfaction which comes from being part of a perfectly executed play. He is not much for wind sprints, sitting on the bench, rainy days, after-game compliments, ankle wraps, scouting reports or calisthenics.

No one else looks forward so much to September or so little to December. Nobody gets so much pleasure out of knocking down, hauling out or just plain bringing down the enemy. Nobody else can cram into one mind assignments for an end run, an off-tackle slant, a play pass, a quarterback sneak, a dive play, punt protection, kick-off returns, a fake punt, four goal line defenses or a reverse designed to result in a touchdown every time it is tried.

continued

A football player is a wonderful creature — you can criticize him, but you can't discourage him. You can defeat his team, but you can't make him quit. You can get him out of a game, but you can't get him out of football. Might as well admit it — be you alumnus, coach or fan — he is your personal representative on the field, your symbol of fair and hard play. He may not be an All-American, but he is an example of the American way. He is judged, not for his race, nor for his religion, but by the democratic yardstick of how well he blocks, tackles, and sacrifices individual glory for the overall success of the team.

He is a hard-working, untiring, determined kid doing the very best he can do for his school or college. And when you come out of a stadium, grousing and feeling upset that your team has lost, he can make you feel mighty ashamed with just two sincerely spoken works — **"WE TRIED."**

* * *

A BOY'S IDOLS

By Stu Brynn
Football Coach, Tabor College (Hillsboro, Kansas)

When I was six years old, I idolized two boys older than I by five and seven years. Both had all the makings of fine athletes. I watched them constantly as they caught a pass, hit a baseball, made a basket and I pictured the day when I would be like them.

It thrilled me to catch a pass thrown by them, a ball pitched by them, or retrieve a basketball shot by them. My day was made when they would say "hello" or simply nod their head in my direction. They were my idols. I longed to be an athlete just like them.

I grew and they grew.

I watched and listened as they bragged about cheating in school. I absorbed all of the ways of cribbing on exams. The hidden answers written on the palm of the hand, the half-opened book on the floor.

I listened as they told of how they took it easy in practice sessions; how they refused to block for a teammate they didn't like; how they chewed Dentyne and rubbed their hands with after-shave lotion so the coach wouldn't know they were smoking.

I listened as they bragged about how many beers they could drink; how many girls they had had; how many nights they had broken curfew.

I listened as they called their mother "old lady" and their father "old man." As they called this teacher and that coach something else; I listened as they spoke of Church and God being non-existent. I listened as they bragged about telling off a teacher; about stealing library books; about stealing equipment from the locker room.

continued

X. WORK * EDUCATION

Boy's Idols *continued*

I listened as they laughed about quitting a team; being thrown off a team; being thrown out of a game for fighting; being thrown out of school.

I listened as they swore. Man, they were the greatest! They were my idols. I longed to be an athlete just like them.

I grew and they grew.

I became a man. Suddenly, I saw my life in perspective. I wondered about my two idols. Surely they were successful; surely they were All-Americans; surely they were pillars of their community.

I searched and I found them. Alas, both had given up struggling to establish themselves as plain, ordinary people. They had set no records; achieved no goals; set no world on fire.

Once I had worshipped them. Now, no one in the community gave them a second look.

Then I wondered; could some young, aspiring athlete have idolized me? Had I led him down the same trail I had followed; had he longed to be an athlete — just like me?

My parents: could I ever repay them for the sorrow and anguish I had brought them? My teachers and coaches: could I ever befriend them? Other people had suffered because of me; could they ever forgive me? That young aspiring athlete; could he forgive me? Where is he now?

They have grown older and so have I.

Now I am a parent. I love my sons deeply. I want them to love God. I want them to serve man. I want them to be athletes.

My sons will watch and listen to you because you are athletes. You will wear the Green and White. Many other sons will watch and listen to you, too. You are their idols. They will long to be athletes just like you. You will grow and they will grow.

Someday you will have sons. Perhaps my sons will be their idols. Your sons will want to be just like them.

* * *

A lot of people love their jobs. It's the work they hate.

* * *

TO GET THE TRUE MEASURE OF A MAN, NOTE HOW MUCH MORE HE DOES THAN IS REQUIRED OF HIM.

X. WORK * EDUCATION

THE BIG GAME

You take the color and the flash of the game,
And the human gardens of rose-lip girls,
And all the pageant that waits the call
As the toe drives into the waiting ball,

But leave me the halfback's driving might,
The surging lines in a bitter fight,
The sweat and smear of the warring soul
As the tackle opens a two-foot hole;
The roar of the crowds, with their breasts aflame,
The ringing cheers, with their eddying swirls,
The interference, the deadly pass,
The grip and crash of the swirling mass.

For the crowd fades out and the cheers dip low
When the fourth down comes, with a yard to go,
And in the struggle along the field
the battle changes to sword and shield
And the knightly tourneys that used to be
In the golden era of chivalry.

The world grows soft as the years advance
Further and further from sword and lance,
When the cavemen, after his morning's fun,
Slew the mammoth and mastodon;
But his ghost at the gridiron calls through space;
"These, too, are worthy to build a race."

* * *

The trouble with the future is that it usually arrives before we are ready for it.

* * *

**It is becoming more and more apparent that we rust out instead of
wear out. Physical and mental activity are vital if we wish to prolong
the youthful portion of life and enjoy later years.**

* * *

A PLAYER'S MIND, LIKE HIS BODY, MUST BE IN CONDITION.

* * *

The Team Man Is The Most Valuable Man On The Team

* * *

Anyone who stops learning is old, whether this happens at 20 or 80.

Henry Ford

IF

If you can keep your head when all about you
    Are losing theirs and blaming it on you;
If you can trust yourself when all men doubt you,
    But make allowance for their doubting too:
If you can wait and not be tired by waiting,
    Or, being lied about, don't deal in lies,
Or being hated don't give way to hating,
    And yet don't look too good, nor talk too wise;

If you can dream—and not make dreams your master;
    If you can think—and not make thoughts your aim,
If you can meet with Triumph and Disaster
    And treat those two imposters just the same:
If you can bear to hear the truth you've spoken
    Twisted by knaves to make a trap for fools,
Or watch the things you gave your life to, broken,
    And stoop and build 'em up with worn-out tools;

If you can make one heap of all your winnings
    And risk it on one turn of pitch-and-toss,
And lose, and start again at your beginnings,
    And never breath a word about your loss:
If you can force your heart and nerve and sinew
    To serve your turn long after they are gone,
And so hold on when there is nothing in you
    Except the Will which says to them: "Hold on!"

If you can talk with crowds and keep your virtue,
    Or walk with Kings — nor lose the common touch,
If neither foes nor loving friends can hurt you,
    If all men count with you, but none too much:
If you can fill the unforgiving minute
    With sixty seconds' worth of distance run,
Yours is the Earth and everything that's in it,
    And — which is more — you'll be a Man, my son!

Rudyard Kipling

* * *

IN MY DREAM . . . . .

I heard some high school teachers cry: "What did they learn in junior high?" But those who teach the seventh grade a different explanation made: "The grade schools simply don't succeed: They never teach them how to read." Each grade school teacher says, "Oh dear; what did she teach 'em all last year?" In first grade with contempt, sublime, we say: "Kindergarten is a mess because parents have failed with readiness. Ah me! The day is almost here, with needles and new pills every year we'll brave the pregnant mother's wrath, and inject pre-natal science and math . . ."

* * *

IF YOU KNOW IT, SHOW IT!

X. WORK * EDUCATION

HALF OF BEING SMART IS KNOWING WHAT YOU'RE DUMB AT.

* * *

A ship in a harbor is safe, but that is not what ships are built for.

* * *

The Game Of Life

To each is given a bag of tools,
A shapeless mass and a book of rules,
And each must fashion ere life is flown,
A stumbling block or a stepping stone.

Isn't is strange that princes and kings
And clowns that caper in sawdust rings
And common folk like you and me,
Are builders of eternity?

* * *

UNLESS YOU TRY TO DO SOMETHING BEYOND WHAT YOU HAVE
ALREADY DONE AND MASTERED, YOU WILL NEVER GROW . . .

* * *

*True Grit is making a decision and standing by it, doing what must
be done — for no moral man can have peace of mind if he leaves un-
done what he knows he should have done.*

John Wayne

* * *

YOU CANNOT DO A KINDNESS TOO SOON BECAUSE YOU NEVER KNOW HOW
SOON IT WILL BE TOO LATE.

RALPH WALDO EMERSON

* * *

I see no virtue where I smell no sweat.

Francis Quarles

* * *

SET YOUR GOAL HIGHER THAN YOU CAN REACH — THEN REACH IT.

GLENN STEWARD

* * *

We can often do more for other men by correcting our own faults than
by trying to correct theirs.